AUTHORITY

AUTHORITY

Strategic Concepts from 15 International Thought
Leaders to Create Influence, Credibility and a
Competitive Edge for You and Your Business

JOHN NORTH

CHRISTINE ROBINSON

MATT SMITH

ADAM JOHNSON

LARRY MORRISON

CATHY FYOCK

ALLAN MCLENNAN

JENN FOSTER

DENISE GABEL

JASON B.A. VAN CAMP

MARK LEONARD

MELANIE JOHNSON

NATHAN JOHNSON

EVERETT O'KEEFE

GEORGE SMOLINSKI

Authority

Strategic Concepts from 15 International Thought Leaders to Create Influence, Credibility and a Competitive Edge for You and Your Business

1st Edition. 2020

ISBN: 978-1-950710-95-9 (Amazon Print)
ISBN: 978-1-950710-96-6 (IngramSpark) PAPERBACK
ISBN: 978-1-950710-97-3 (IngramSpark) HARDCOVER
ISBN: 978-1-950710-98-0 (E-book)
Library of Congress Control Number: 2020918169

CONTACT THE PUBLISHER:

Business Name: Ignite Publishing
Author Website: www.authoritythebook.com
Main Website: www.ignitepress.us

TRADEMARKS

This book is dedicated to those who are authorities in their field and especially to those who don't know it yet.

Acknowledgements

A book is always a team effort, but this book is much more so. This is a collaborative effort between experts in the publishing industry and beyond, and some gratitude is due to the many players who did their part.

We would like to thank the following:

The authors who contributed their time and expertise through their contributions.

The members of the Business Accelerator Group, whose participation (official and unofficial) not only led to the inception of this project but also helped refine and polish it along the way.

Cathy Fyock, who shepherded all of our authors through the writing and editing process.

Our editor, Eileen Ansel Conery, for catching and correcting our foibles and mistakes.

Elite Online Publishing, Ignite Press, Gutenberg Reloaded, and Evolvepreneur.app for the many "in kind" contributions to this project.

The Authors

John North

Evolvepreneur.app CEO & Founder, Strategic Marketer and Book Publisher

 https://www.linkedin.com/in/johnnorth1085

 https://www.facebook.com/johnnorthauthor

 https://twitter.com/johnnorth7

 https://johnnorth.com.au

Christine Robinson

Empress On Fire - Leading Transformational Teacher and 6+ Figure Strategist

 https://www.facebook.com/christinerob

 https://www.facebook.com/likechristine

 https://www.instagram.com/publisherchristinerobinson/

 http://christinerobinson.com.au

Matt Smith
Cereal Dad-Preneur

 https://www.facebook.com/profile.php?id=1632326310

 https://www.instagram.com/mattsmithpueblo/

 www.cerealdadpreneur.com/book

Adam Johnson
Real Estate Investor and Educator

 https://www.facebook.com/wholesalehackers

 https://www.facebook.com/groups/realestateroundup

 https://www.instagram.com/bigsiprealestate/

Larry Morrison
Founder/CEO of College Loan Freedom

 https://www.linkedin.com/in/larry-morrison

 https://www.facebook.com/collegeloanfreedom

 http://bit.ly/CLFVid

 https://www.collegeloanfreedom.com/

Cathy Fyock, CSP, SPHR, SHRM-SCP
The Business Book Strategist

 https://www.linkedin.com/in/cathy-fyock-973b735/

 https://www.facebook.com/TheBusinessBookStrategist/

 https://twitter.com/CathyFyock

 https://www.cathyfyock.com/

Allan McLennan, p.g.a.
Chief Executive, PADEM Media Group/USA, Global Streaming Media Market Developer, Technologist & Analyst

 https://www.linkedin.com/in/allannmclennan/

 www.pademmediagroup.com/books

Jenn Foster
15X Bestselling Author

 https://www.linkedin.com/in/jennfosterseo

 https://www.facebook.com/authorjennfoster/

 https://www.instagram.com/jennfosterchic

 https://authorjennfoster.com/

Denise Gabel

High Trust Environment – Author, Speaker, and Professional Advisor

 https://www.linkedin.com/in/denise-gabel-5010794/

 http://thedenise.com/

Jason B.A. Van Camp

Business Growth Strategist

 https://www.linkedin.com/in/jason-van-camp-076a5339/

 www.missionsixzero.com

 www.warriorrising.org

Mark Leonard

Book Coach

 linkedin.com/in/markcleonard

 https://CartwrightPublishing.com

Melanie Johnson
Publishing, Marketing and Brand Expert

 https://www.linkedin.com/in/melaniejohnson-eop/

 https://www.instagram.com/eliteonlinepublishing/

 https://www.youtube.com/watch?v=aXyLNrnl70E

 https://eliteonlinepublishing.com/

Nathan Johnson
Social Media Advertising and Brand Specialist

 https://www.instagram.com/weekdayrehab/

Everett O'Keefe
International #1 Bestselling Author, Publishing Expert, Founder of Ignite Press

 https://www.linkedin.com/company/ignite-press (Company)

 https://www.linkedin.com/in/everettokeefe/ (Personal)

 https://www.facebook.com/ignitepress

 https://IgnitePress.us

George Smolinski

Founder, Gutenberg Reloaded

 https://www.facebook.com/GutenbergReloaded

 https://www.youtube.com/channel/UCF_9iLkvxcYlv-c_PcKP50Q

 www.gutenbergreloaded.com

Table of Contents

Introduction

AUTHORITY is a loaded term. It is filled with meaning that few of us fully understand, but most interpret authority as someone who has the right to give orders or someone in control. Although the word contains "author" as its root, its meaning is not limited to *authorship* in the traditional sense. Authority goes so much further. In fact, authority and author each find their origins in the Latin word: *augere.* In the strictest sense, *augere* means "to increase," but the term also came to mean *to honor or exalt, to promote or raise,* and *to augment.* In time, the word morphed into "autor," that is, *creator* and *one who executes.* In the 14th century, these roots (and these meanings) finally coalesced into the words we know: author, authentic, and authority.

Authority, you see, is not about writing. It is first and foremost about *creating.* The genesis of authority is in the inception of ideas. These can be new ideas or they can be ideas that have been gathered and melded into something unique. The author (meaning, the creator) of such ideas is, by default, the authority on the subject.

Although we tend to think this is true only with the creation of novel ideas or at least a "new take" on old ideas, the truth is that authority also is granted for those who can repackage or repurpose that which already was known. Oftentimes, the so-called expert is simply the person who happens to bring the right information to the right person at the right time. This does not necessarily require a new, astounding way to look at a subject.

The creation that leads to authority is not limited to any one particular medium either. Although authorship of books often is cited as a path to authority, such authority can be gained through creation in any medium. As such, you will find "authorities" on every subject under the sun, from history and politics to sports and crafts. The creation that leads to such authority can come from almost anything.

In these pages, you will find 15 expert perspectives spanning three different continents. These authors come from diverse backgrounds, with entirely different professions and skillsets, and they share their unique observations on authority, what it means, how to acquire it, and how to leverage it.

At the beginning of each chapter, we have included information about the respective author as well as ways you can contact or follow the author. We encourage you to learn more about the authors; engage with them where you see fit.

It is our collective hope you will find the perspectives in *Authority* to be enlightening and useful. More than this, we hope the lessons of *Authority* will take root and bear fruit in your life.

CHAPTER 1

The Future of Online Entrepreneurs

John North

Evolvepreneur.app CEO & Founder,
Strategic Marketer and Book Publisher

 https://www.linkedin.com/in/johnnorth1085

 https://www.facebook.com/johnnorthauthor

 https://twitter.com/johnnorth7

 https://johnnorth.com.au

John North is a Seven-Time #1 International Best-Selling Author who is regarded as a versatile and experienced entrepreneur with a solid background in Accounting, Banking, Business Management, Finance, Personal Development, IT, Software and Strategic Marketing.

John has written six #1 Best Selling Books about book publishing, business strategy, and internet marketing and as well a book about Squash.

John is the CEO of Evolve Systems Group. He is a serial entrepreneur who has created many products and services that are designed to empower business owners and entrepreneurs.

Some of these ventures include: Evolve Global Publishing, Evolvepreneur.app, Evolvepreneur.club, Evolve Your Business, and Evolve Mobile.

John's passion is to help business owners become smarter and more strategic about their marketing efforts. He constantly pushes the envelope of what's possible in this modern era and is widely regarded among his peers as very innovative and highly creative in his approach.

His latest venture is Evolvepreneur.app. It is an all-in-one platform designed to allow entrepreneurs to take control of their future and to be less reliant on using social media for managing their business online.

John lives in Sydney, Australia with his wife and son and plays competitive squash 5 days a week.

• • •

Never in the history of the modern world has it been easier to start your own business — especially online.

My journey to entrepreneurship, and generating more than $25 million in revenue to date is certainly an interesting and varied one.

After leaving school at age 15, I started my first job as a bank employee in a small country town. Throughout the next 12 years, my roles in the bank included: front office, supervision, legal, and lending. I learned many skills while at the bank, including management, systems, and procedures, as well as how to handle unhappy customers!

Along the way, I trained as an ambulance and state emergency services officer. I even received an Australia Day award for services to the local community.

In 1989, I started getting very interested in the emerging computer revolution and founded a part-time computer and accounting software business. I soon realized the huge opportunity emerging, so I resigned from the bank and started working full-time. In a few years, it quickly grew to more than $1.5 million per year in recurring revenues.

In 2000, Australia introduced a new sales tax "GST" system and my business went from boom to bust — the new tax drove businesses to computerize en masse for the reporting they needed to do, and it sucked all new revenue from future years.

I faced my first major business failure and was forced to close the business, but was fortunate enough to get a new job working as the CEO for my accounting software supplier in Sydney.

After six months of being an employee, I made a successful bid to take over their Australian operations as their sole distributor and become a self-employed entrepreneur again. Within a few years, with annual revenues in excess of $2.5 million (nearly 80% recurring) we became #2 in the world for a major accounting software brand.

I learned a lot about developing recurring revenue, software development, negotiation, marketing, sales, and people management throughout those years.

In 2013, I sold the distribution company to focus on my new venture, Evolve Systems, providing digital marketing services for clients. Along the way, I became a hybrid book publisher and was involved in publishing more than 2,000 books.

My next venture will draw on all of my previous experience and then some!

The internet certainly has changed the world and made it easier to start a new business, but not everything has changed. In reality, the true art of business hasn't changed significantly. The way people decide what to buy is much the same as it always has been.

What has changed is the volume of information a prospect can uncover and how quickly they can research their options.

With the rise of social media platforms, it has become so easy to generate interest for your product or service by creating a social media page, running some ads, and writing posts to accumulate likes. You even can create a special interest group to attract conversations with your best buyers. Many businesses today are only present on social platforms but do not have a website.

These platforms deliberately make it easy for you to outsource your customers to them, while simultaneously restricting the information you need to contact them later.

With the recent push for individual privacy protections and better government regulation for Big Tech, these social media platforms are now pulling the ladder up behind them and keeping the majority of the meaningful data for themselves.

These social media platforms might be free and easy to use, but they come with a cost — and it's something that many online businesses don't see until it's too late. Accumulating likes and followers on social media is a bit like renting a nice apartment. It's clean and fancy, but it's not really yours.

If you break any of their rules — both the reasonable and the draconian — you risk losing access to your followers by being banned or blocked. In fact, they often penalize posts that contain off-site web links, because they don't want their users leaving their site. Past a certain point, this stops being a symbiotic relationship and starts costing you more than you're earning. You hit a ceiling, and you need to break past it if you want to grow your business.

On top of this, the cost of advertising on these platforms is only going up, because the majority of their customers are now big corporations.

What does this all mean to you?

As a time-poor, typically underfunded online entrepreneur who receives so much conflicting advice about the best ways to grow your business, how can you compete with the big end of town without any of the resources they have at their disposal?

Let's imagine that you send some traffic to your social profiles.

You should then focus on building a closer relationship with your prospects by moving them from that site to your own community platform.

Notice I didn't say website.

Let me explain what a community platform means for an online entrepreneur.

The major challenge that most online business owners face is providing a world-class website experience since it can be complicated and expensive. It often means cobbling several solutions together using plugins and third-party tools to get a functioning website capable of engaging and convincing visitors to buy from you.

As the number of businesses relying on the internet for day-to-day operations has grown, a new type of software system has arisen. It's called SaaS – Software as a Service.

I remember when I first started selling accounting software – you often had to buy multiple unconnected products to manage your cashbook, invoicing, payroll, and asset management. Over time, these functions merged into powerful, interconnected single-system solutions at a fraction of the cost of all the individual components.

Individually, these systems often are costly and labor-intensive to maintain. When I started working for clients in digital marketing, if I ran into a problem, I knew there was "an app for that". Whilst this is great, it also opens your business up to problems if one app fails or someone misses an update or forgets to sync all of these unconnected applications.

I believe the next-level SaaS "social platform" or "all-in-one business system" will be a significant opportunity in the marketplace for entrepreneurs.

If you want to create a real growth-based sustainable business, my advice is to focus on building your own complete system; become independent from "Big Tech" so you can't be banned or throttled. Use them to send traffic to your own assets like a website, recurring membership, online e-commerce shop, or e-learning platform, and build your own audience.

As a marketing consultant, after thousands of hours of consulting and deploying marketing systems, the following is a blueprint for what I believe a typical online entrepreneur needs to be successful in today's highly-competitive marketplace:

- Your major focus should be the overall customer experience. You will also want to try to be as frictionless as possible throughout. At the same time, employ as much automation as possible.

- You should start with a mobile-ready website that tightly integrates your content-based assets, such as your podcast channel, on-demand videos, courses, memberships and blogs.

- Seamlessly build up your subscriber database and automatically email subscribers when new content is available. Your marketing module should trigger emails or actions based on your prospect's behavior, as well as help them progress through your courses and products.

- You will need to design some pages to promote free checklists, blueprints, and/or ebooks to build your subscriber database. You will want your visitors to be able to buy your products & services and handle the delivery of your digital download or physical product on the same site. At the same time, you may wish to upsell products at checkout. By segmenting your prospects, you can build powerful followup emails.

- You should have multiple payment gateways. This reduces the risk of one portal withholding funds if you grow too fast. You could also sell products in different currencies to lower buyer resistance.

- You may want the ability to create a recurring membership system where you can charge users at regular intervals and allow them to easily update their records with you.

- You may want different front-end websites, but they should all lead back to your eCommerce and backend member area so you can manage them easily. This allows you to promote different angles of your business without splitting up your audience or resources.

- To grow your business, you should create an affiliate program and encourage referrers or affiliates to share your products and services for rewards.

- At the end of the process, the prospect or customer should finish their initial journey in your back-end membership area, which includes all of their invoices, downloads, and bonus content. You don't want your customers fumbling around with separate websites looking for all of this information!

- It's vital to have a ticketing system or similar service system to support your customers.

- The next step is to create a highly-engaged community for your clients and prospects that provides extra value behind a secure login and keeps them coming back for your content.

- To further engage users, you need to gamify your community through status badges and rewards systems.

- Think about creating courses where your members can learn online at their own pace. Your course system should allow them to progress step-by-step as they do each lesson, not necessarily on a weekly release schedule where they could quickly get behind and give up. You should also encourage students to engage with other students.

- What if they didn't need to download a worksheet PDF they never actually complete? You need a system to allow them to leave their responses as they work through the lessons. This will give you the ability to see all their answers, which means you also know where they are in the course. This means no one is left behind!

- A useful feature is to be able to assign a task to your students as they progress through the course. You could also create a coaching program based on their task list.

- You also need a powerful analytics reporting system that tells you exactly where your traffic is coming from and what they're clicking on to help make decisions for your marketing campaigns.

- You will also want a single dashboard to view statistics, create content, and manage your business.

- Ideally, you should build a procedure system (Knowledge Base) so your staff and outsourcers can run your processes the same way every time. Make it easy to create step-by-step instructions rather than having to continually re-train staff.

- What if you wanted to create a mastermind group? It would be best if you could group people together and allow users to be able to access Q&A calls, group tasks, and results in a logical and centralized way.

- It would also help to have a project management system to help you and your team manage your projects as well as client ones.

- Most importantly, your platform needs to have fast loading times, or you risk driving customers away!

How long do you think it would take to implement all of this?

Maybe a year or longer!

I've spent thousands of dollars and many fruitless hours in search of the best all-in-one platform that had most of the features I wanted. But as far as I could tell, that system doesn't exist. In frustration, I set out on a journey to develop my own unique platform, completely based around the needs of entrepreneurs, coaches, consultants, authors, podcasters, publishers, and mastermind groups.

I called it evolvepreneur.app. My mission is to start a revolution to help entrepreneurs establish their own complete business system that can compete with mainstream social media platforms.

Don't become a cog in the machine; create your own machine.

I challenge you to focus on building your own complete business community platform.

Take control of your destiny and sleep better a night!

CHAPTER 2

I Help Fulfill Dreams! Create A Legacy, Impact, and Income

Empress On Fire - Leading Transformational
Teacher and 6+ Figure Strategist

 https://www.facebook.com/christinerob

 https://www.facebook.com/likechristine

 https://www.instagram.com/publisherchristinerobinson/

http://christinerobinson.com.au

'Empress On Fire', Christine is on a mission to assist passion-driven entrepreneurs and thought leaders turn their messages into bestselling books. Through her mentoring and proven strategies, she takes budding authors from having a simple idea to being recognized as extraordinary experts in their field.

An international #1 bestselling author and speaker, Christine not only helps leaders become bestselling authors, but she also helps them create a holistic (the ONE Thing) range of offers, including high-end packages and experiences, along with more passive and leveraged offers. Supporting clients to create massive impact, income, and influence through automated systems and their speaking, media, and further publishing opportunities.

More than 20 years of teaching experience and bundles of sales experience gives Christine the ability to deliver highly valuable coaching and training in a way that suits all learning styles, resulting in high success rates.

Christine can be found organizing luxurious retreats, leading seminars, and working with clients from around the world, all from her office in the beautiful Barossa Valley, South Australia (great wine country), where she lives with her husband Chris and furry friend Winston.

You can access your own 'Six-Figure Author Toolkit' here: www.empressonfire.com/toolkit

I love helping to fulfill dreams! I not only help fulfill dreams, but also help many business owners gain clarity in their purpose, gain focus, and take massive action towards their dreams.

Did you know that around 88% of the U.S. population dreams of writing a book, but only 2% ever do? And of that 2%, only 1% become a #1 best-selling author. Authorship to me has many different meanings; authoring a book, authoring and publishing content, or more importantly, it is having an exquisite vision, like many of my book clients, that can be life-changing for so many people. They have an inner knowing, a powerful pull, a powerful energy that drives them to do what they do and they have a strong desire to help transform the lives of others. I have that pull and you probably have it too. Otherwise, you wouldn't be reading this book!

VISION

Authorship is about your *Why* and connecting to your purpose and to your unique story in a way that manifests in great possibilities for both the author and the reader. I truly believe that entrepreneurs are the ones who are going to lead the future and they are the ones who have the creativity and the innovation to do it. There has never been a better time to get your message out to the market, to *Magnify Your Message.*

Simon Sinek said that most business owners and most employees can easily explain what they do and how they do it, but few can explain why they do it. They're unable to explain their mission, their purpose, and why they're doing what they're doing.

One of my coaches said, "There are three steps to true greatness." These three steps are:

1. Your connectedness to your *Why*, to your vision
2. Having confidence and clarity in your ability to deliver your vision
3. Take massive, imperfect action consistently

Through the writing process, you connect with your *Why*. Also with the why of your reader (or you should). When written correctly, your book should help your reader to connect with your vision, while seeing the possibilities for themselves. You start by really stepping into your Dream Client or reader's mind, with what keeps them awake at night and how you can help them solve their most pressing problems. You get to know them better than they know themselves and while reading they think *'that's me you're talking about,'* or *'get out of my mind.'* You're seen as the Authority and are able to attract highly targeted clients to you. Your book can open many doors and is a great way to leverage your time.

We all know that the two most important things in this world are time and money and that we can never get our time back; it is limited. I'm going to share with you how, by focusing on your book as the one thing, you can make more impact and more money while leveraging your time.

We're in the era of sales 3.0. Sales 1.0 was where you were taught to change a product's features into benefits. Think of the features being logic and benefits the emotion. Then from around 2008, we had Sales 2.0 and attraction marketing being taught by Seth Godin and others. Always an early adopter, I taught a lot about attraction marketing within my social media business. It was so easy to stand out from the crowd back then, but nowadays most business people online understand the need for attraction marketing.

So, that brings us to today and Sales 3.0 where selling is an ARTform:

- Authority
- Results
- Trust

Authority to be seen, heard, found, read, and respected in the marketplace; and to be seen as the expert, as the authority. By authoring a book, and in particular a best seller, you automatically establish your authority in your niche or marketplace. Just think back to any seminars or speaker events you may have attended. What's the first thing the emcee usually states as they introduce the next speaker? "Jane Smith, international best-selling author" or similar. Are you ready for a speaking engagement or a TV appearance?

Results — to make great sales and attract the right people you need to demonstrate the results that you, your product, or service can help them achieve. You can accomplish this by sprinkling stories and case studies of your results, your client results, or borrowed results from a third party. Two clients of mine, Rhonda and Ryan, did this extremely well. Rhonda shared stories and testimonials while helping her readers see how she can help them, too. Ryan used a free plus shipping funnel with free tickets to his events inside his book. From there he sold more than 50% of the room into a $4,000 or $8,000 program. So, your book also creates great ROI, when used in this way.

Another R that happens with your book is that you build relationships with your readers. Have you ever read a book where you can picture and hear the author? In some cases, you feel like you know them intimately.

Trust for people to know, like, and trust you. That is where we are with sales right now, people no longer want to buy from big brands. They want to buy from people who they know, like, and trust, as well as those they see as the authority and who can demonstrate results they achieved for themselves or for others. Another way to build trust is through testimonials. Authors often share these inside the book or in the book description and cover. So, your book helps you in all these areas. It shows that you are the authority, you can get results, and you can build trust.

Harriet was only 25 when I helped her write her book, *Be Your Best*. The week after her launch, a reader rang her up, wanting to work with her, and paid her $2,000.

YOUR ONE THING

In the book *The One Thing*, Gary Keller and Jay Papasan identified that behind every successful person is their ONE Thing. That ONE Thing stands between you and your goals, and it helps you achieve extraordinary results in every situation. You probably know about the Pareto Principle, the 80/20 rule, where 20% of your efforts gives you 80% of your results. In *The ONE Thing*, Gary asks you to drill down even further and ask yourself and define, "what is the ONE Thing that you can do in your life that will provide the biggest progress and the biggest growth?"

One of the myths that Gary dispels is that of multitasking. Now, I've always been proud of being able to multitask, being the woman that I am, that is until I saw research into how it really can hold one back. I discovered how I could reach goals so much faster and become much more productive once I started focusing on the ONE Thing.

Your ONE Thing may be a particular goal for which you're striving, or it may be how to build amazing businesses while being an amazing Dad, like my client Matt. For many of my clients, their first or next book is their ONE Thing. Using their book as their vehicle of choice to create more impact and more income, while helping more people.

Earlier I mentioned Simon Sinek's *Why* talk and how your book can help your reader envision your *why* as well as their *why*; you show them the what, and a bit of the how. Some will be able to take your ideas and solutions and run with them, but most will need more, they will need some hand-holding or accountability, and therefore they need you! Your book is the tip of the iceberg where you take your reader through the start of their customer journey with you. Your customer's journey being: awareness, interest, desire, and action.

While reading your book, or even the blurb as they pick it up in-store, your reader becomes aware that they have a problem. They are now interested to find out more and perhaps click on your book bonus link or visit your website to find out more about you and how you can help solve their problem. They now see what is possible for them, and for those with an urgent enough desire or need, they will take action and engage with your products and services.

OR

You can model the best of the best, such as Tony Robbins, Brené Brown, Brendon Burchard, Russell Brunson, Gina DeVee, and now my clients. No doubt you will know how a sales funnel works, how you build awareness through social media content, videos, podcast interviews (organic), or Facebook ads (paid), and from there invite them to take some sort of action and convert it into a sale. As I mentioned earlier, one of the fastest ways to grow your business is to use your book to build that awareness. Just like Tony Robbins and many others, your book is the front end (tip of the iceberg) of your funnel — either free plus shipping, or under $30 — and from there you bring them through your highly sophisticated funnel where you offer other products or services in your value ladder (see later).

SIX-PLUS-FIGURE BOOK EMPIRE

The following are two examples of how this might work:

One1 Free Plus Shipping

You may have seen this funnel advertised often on Facebook by the likes of Tony Robbins, Brendon Burchard, and Russell Brunson.

Step One — advertise your soft copybook for free (or low lost) plus shipping and handling. This is called a self-liquidating offer (SLO), that means the revenue is just about equal to the ad costs. The customer fills out the delivery and credit card details.

Step Two — you are offered a 'bump' or a no brainer offer, which many you are likely to take for an additional $27 or $37 for example.

Step Three — you then are then offered to upsell one, upsell two, maybe a down-sell.

Step Four — thank you page and your book is on its way to the buyer—you!

These are highly valuable funnels, as research shows, that approximately 25% of buyers will move from Step One to Step Two, and so on. The relationship develops and the customer can become a client and move up the value ladder... or jump straight to the top.

Two2 Low Cost Plus shipping

This is a fast and highly successful method one of my coaches is using. Ben made an additional six-plus- figures from his book funnel in less than six months.

Step One — Facebook ads with a video clip of his book.

Step Two — Mail out books, within three to four days.

Step Three — Call purchasers — they were so amazed and impressed that the author was calling.

Step Four — Ask questions — he simply asked them what they liked and with what they were struggling most in their business (substitute business for health, relationships, etc.).

Step Five — Invite them to a strategy call — these were the easiest sales calls as his book was an ARTform.

When I first start working with new clients, I love seeing their excitement when they discover how they can use their book-writing process to map out and design their whole value or ascension ladder, then easily and quickly create six- to 12-months content to attract awareness.

Through the mapping out exercise, we focus on the ONE Thing to outline the chapters for their books, online course, group, and one-on-one coaching, mentorship, and many other possibilities for their ascension ladder. You can find out more about this through the links in my bio.

"80% Of Winning Is Showing Up"

— Woody Allen

You've bought this book, now go and share your message, become one of the 2%, make more money and impact... it's time to...

Go Be Extraordinary!

CHAPTER 3

It's Going to be a Good Day!

Matt Smith

Cereal Dad-Preneur

 https://www.facebook.com/profile.php?id=1632326310

 https://www.instagram.com/mattsmithpueblo/

 www.cerealdadpreneur.com/book

Selling gum, running paper routes, and mowing lawns was the start of Matt Smith's entrepreneurial career. Today Matt is Founder and owner of many businesses including Snooze Mattress Company, the largest Snap Fitness (Pueblo) in the world, Wakeup Marketing, and a commercial and residential real estate investor and developer. Matt has started and sold 5 other businesses in completely different industries and has a genuine love and passion for business and its people.

A Pueblo, Colorado native, Matt is engaged with various community organizations. and is a mentor for Fellowship of Christian Athletes. He and wife Jenny have three wonderful children; Parker 6, Paisley 5, and Preston almost 2 years old. Matt's family is his WHY, his driving force. His daily habits and choices revolve around his family and having fun both at home and at work. In his bestselling book Cereal Dad-Preneur, Matt shares many lessons and stories to help entrepreneurs balance wealth building, work, and family as much as possible. While there is never complete balance, Matt and Jenny ensure that they spend out of school hours together and take many family trips to their mountain home and trips overseas.

Matt can be reached at mattsmith.pueblo@gmail.com

I am a fast action taker in all areas of my life... I make decisions fast, I buy real estate fast, I buy businesses fast, I sell businesses fast, I speak fast, and I really don't overthink anything, I just move into action fast. But, there's one thing I've wanted to do for more than five years, and this may have been one of the most intimidating things I ever have done — to write my book and become an author. However, I love a good challenge and knew my first book would be the hardest. Hopefully, after the first one is completed, I could start making fast decisions on a book the next time.

What was holding me back? It was my belief that I was not a writer and that my ADHD inhibited me from being able to write a book. A book that I knew in my heart would help transform the lives of so many busy parents, and in particular, business owners. Even though I had this burning desire to write my book, my fear of not being a good enough writer was stopping me, that is until COVID-19 hit. The massive shutdown completely altered our daily schedules and our very way of life. This interruption in my typical routine created, among other things, the window of time for me to finish writing my first book. So, I did what I do best and hired a publishing team to extract my message and my experiences to write *Cereal Dad-Preneur*.

Being an entrepreneur was in my blood from an early age. I started my adventure in the business world in grade school, selling gum out of my locker, mowing lawns, and running paper routes to make money. Today, I consider myself a *Serial Entrepreneur.* I have created and developed at least 10 different businesses, all of which continue to grow and thrive in my amazing, but small hometown of Pueblo, Colorado. In fact, while writing my book, I also created a marketing business and bought the oldest building in my community with the intent to turn it into a movement to #wakeup and promote our community.

The most surprising thing about my endeavors is that they are each in different industries. Since I was not an expert in any of them, the key to my success was developing systems that worked across diverse industries.

While I am proud that I've busted my butt and earned everything I have, I'm also grateful and blessed beyond belief. Writing this book has challenged me on many levels, but sharing my stories and writing about what I've achieved in my life, tested me more than I expected. My coach kept reminding me that telling my story isn't about bragging; it's about helping my reader see that I have the expertise and proven success to help them achieve their dream. And, if I can do it, they can too!

FAMILY FIRST

People often ask me, "What motivates you?" My wife, Jenny, and my three children, Parker, Paisley, and Preston are my driving force and my "BIG WHY". Growing up as the son of a single mom, I had the opportunity to see the struggles and triumphs of putting family first while working full-time. My mom, Kathy Jean Luke, was amazing and taught me that parenting is the most loving journey you will ever take. She may not have had a lot of money, but what my mom lacked in funds, she more than made up for in love for her family.

My intent with *Cereal Dad-Preneur* (I love the play on words as breakfast time is one of my favorite times of the day, spent with my kids) is to present readers a road map and a practical guide to achieving success in all areas of their lives. I hope they take away golden nuggets; such as how to build exceptional systems, boost communication, manage or bend time, grow their positivity muscle, and take control of their health, to name a few.

Another reason for writing this book is to leave a legacy for my children, as well as their children. To give them insight into what has been going on throughout their early childhood.

My family is my WHY. They are what drive Jenny and me to create the businesses we do. While I'm by no means perfect, I feel so blessed to live the life I do, to have the people in my life that I do, in our local community of Pueblo, and my family at work. I play hard at work, as well as at home. I created my day around being totally present and available. Each and every team member in each of our businesses is family. Lockdown helped us all to become so much closer (during personal growth activities I ran with my teams while we were all at home) and know and understand each other from the heart. My core values are family, raising good humans, taking time to enjoy life, and creating the best memories possible.

BOOK EXCERPT

"FAMILY FIRST has always been my motto, but that doesn't have to come at the expense of pursuing your ambitions and passions of being wildly successful in business at the same time. You CAN have it all and feel good about yourself and your achievements.

I'm not perfect, but I continue to grow and improve every day. Everyone is on a journey, and I want to save the "Dad-Preneur" in you a massive amount of time and effort. What if I could propel you along the learning curve to a place light-years ahead of where you are now, by helping you benefit from my life experiences while bypassing some of my challenges? When you study these lessons and implement the tools and techniques provided, you will develop the systems you need to succeed in any industry, allowing you to work smarter. I promise it will change your life for the better...

Don't let another day go by without taking action to grab hold of the balanced life you and your family deserve. Accelerate your journey to success. Let me teach you the secrets that allowed me to retire in my 30's. Open your mind, roll up your sleeves, and get to work on you!"

Throughout my life, I have had many great mentors and people who have inspired me, beginning with my Mom. Adam Graham was a mentor of mine growing up. He saw my potential and recruited me for a job in the sales department at the Denver Mattress Company. Within the first year, while I was still only 19 years old, I was promoted to Assistant Manager of the Colorado Springs store.

During my 18 years with Denver Mattress, I was fortunate to have one of the most amazing mentors, Darrell Bain. He was and continues to be one of the most influential men in my life. He taught me to love the sales process, be a person of integrity, and earn, rather than demand the respect of my team members. Within two years, at age 21, I was the manager of the Pueblo store. During this time, I found a way to start investing in real estate and set my sights on building a life of which both my mother and grandmother would be proud.

Two years ago, I retired from being an "employee" and I have never looked back. I have sold some businesses and started others, making life so, so exciting.

The start of my day is the most important time to me, it is the only time of which I have complete control. It actually starts the night before, by going to bed by 8:30 pm with meditation music, and having a really good sleep. Sleep is so important to me that I built my own Snooze mattress company. I am also researching and have a team building a meditation pillow and headband.

My day starts at 4:30 am with some cardio exercise while listening to a podcast, or an audiobook, anything that lifts me up and inspires me. Between 6 and 7 am, I catch up on emails, research, and get ready for the day ahead. By 7 am my family is getting up and I just love this part of the day. It is top priority for me to spend breakfast time with my wife and children before taking them to school or daycare. Between 9 am and 5 pm, it's usual office hours and with many businesses — all in close proximity. I completely wear one hat at a time. While I am in each business, I am fully present and engaged in that business and its people. At 5 pm I put my father hat on, pick up my kids, and I'm in total dad mode. After their bedtime, it is husband mode. Whichever hat I'm wearing it is my wish that everyone has fun and has a strong mutual respect for each other.

In Chapter 7 — Who's On Your Bus? I share the importance of people, culture, and systems. We do our utmost to build up team members and provide systems and processes that support the whole team. In Chapter 4, we look at the art of communication. Such an important skill in the workplace, and even more so at home. I share some cute and funny stories involving my kids around communication and positivity.

Positivity is so important to me, and I see it as part of your health regime, by planning to build your positivity muscle each and every day, you will soon reap the benefits and be on your way to reaching your goals. You most certainly attract what you think about and a big game I play with my kids is around *Having a Great Day!* In fact, I have also written a children's book by that name.

THE WRITING PROCESS

The journey into authorship has been a blast. Due to my desire to author my own book, but not 'write' it, Christine and her team interviewed me to extract my story and 'genius' as she calls it. The whole process was so much fun and as I read the proof and read my life in words, I thought 'Boy, this was fun!' — meaning my life so far.

Authority was one of the main reasons for writing my book and already people have been stopping me in the street asking where they can buy it.

During the writing process, I had an LA TV crew follow me almost 24/7, for four months. It has been so exciting to know that in three months' time, I will be in a 12-week Discovery show. I have proudly been dropping comments about my book wherever possible. Always the salesperson!! :)

As I mentioned, working with great mentors and coaches help to catapult your personal and business growth forward at a rapid pace. During the writing process, my coach helped me envision what else is possible and how I can help other parent-preneurs to have wildly successful businesses while balancing family life. More videos, group coaching and immersive retreats will soon be happening. Check the links out in my bio if you'd like to know more.

My advice to you is: if you're thinking of writing your book, just do it. Hire a coach or a publishing team and get it done fast! You will gain clarity, focus, and see how much you can transform the lives of others through sharing your story. The process also helps you explore other avenues to help your readers, such as online courses, or for example, immersive retreats for families, of which I'm currently planning.

CHAPTER 4

Belief is Powerful

Adam Johnson

Real Estate Investor and Educator

https://www.facebook.com/wholesalehackers

https://www.facebook.com/groups/realestateroundup

https://www.instagram.com/bigsiprealestate/

Adam Johnson is the co-founder of both the Facebook Group Real Estate Roundup, Wholesale Hackers YouTube channel, and the Hattiesburg-Area Real Estate Investors Group, focusing on house wholesaling, land buying, and real estate investing education.

He also has spoken to numerous Real Estate Investment groups and has been featured on podcasts, such as CarrotCast, BiggerPockets, and Wholesaling Houses Elite. Between online mentoring and live events, Real Estate Roundup and Wholesale Hackers have helped thousands of beginner, intermediate, and experienced real estate investors grow their portfolio, scale up their business, generate leads, and proactively invest in their business to be able to quit the nine to five grind.

Raised in Mississippi, Adam "Big Sip" Johnson is one of the best educators in negotiating, creative financing, and wholesaling real estate. His techniques have helped many businesses across the country hit new milestones and become viable businesses for their owners.

Along the way to becoming a real estate authority, he founded insurance, tax, and restaurant businesses. In insurance, his agency grew by double digits each year and received the biggest bonus check paid out in the state of Mississippi for his parent company. Owning a tax preparation business, it grew the number of clients and revenue by more than 20%.

He now makes his home in Southern Mississippi with his fiancée Kathryn Grace, and is focused on growing his platforms and businesses in the wholesaling and rental housing markets.

Wow! Did you read that bio? There are better ones out there, to be sure... But, mine's not too shabby. I felt pretty good about it, too. To be honest, I felt pretty good about myself. It'd be easy, in my shoes, to think that all those successes in the past would somehow create a strong individual. Seasoned. Hardened. Tough.

But, after so much success in business and life (or so I thought), I still had some lessons to learn. I thought I was flying high, but it all came crashing down. My world had been turned upside down. I had reached a point where I had lost all belief. Whereas, in my old life I felt like I was on autopilot, cruising to success. When I rediscovered my belief in myself, I found that even though I thought I was successful, I actually wasn't. Along the way, I also found out living with authority and purpose means being in the service of others.

And that's the story I want to share — how I went from zero belief to living a life of which I can be proud, that is hopeful, purposeful, and successful.

I'm not sure there's a soul among us who hasn't had, at least to some degree, a feeling of being lost. Actually, maybe worse than lost in a world where we don't even recognize ourselves anymore. For me personally, it was the exact opposite feeling from what I had imagined my life would feel like. We all picture ourselves successful, great family, best in class, and confident! *'One day!'* we say to ourselves... *'one day!'* The problem was, on this particular day, I had lost all hope of getting there.

Belief is powerful. Before we can begin to do, we must believe.

And in your life, there were or will be times where you may have lost belief in yourself. I know I have.

I can remember the time when I had lost all belief in myself. When I thought I could not go lower.

It was mid-morning. Sometime in June. I could not have been more embarrassed — deeply embarrassed. Ashamed might even be a more appropriate word. That kind of feeling that causes those sleepless nights. I'd been waking up in cold sweats, wondering what kind of future I possibly could shape for myself now?

I'd just watched my car, basically the last of my possessions, get repossessed, and it would seem that tow truck drove off with what little bit of my pride was left as well. I'd lost my businesses, my money, and my self-worth.

My car being towed away was the latest in a line of failures when just a few years before I thought I had the Midas Touch.

I was on the top of the world I thought, only to see it go away. So, square one and I are well acquainted. But, even with losing everything as I did, the first story I'd like to share is how I found my way back.

My entire life had just slipped through my fingers. But, even at my lowest and thinking, I lost everything, I had people who still believed in me. Even when I thought I had lost everything, I still had my relationships. So, even if you're at square one, you have something. When I was down, I talked to my dad. We had a conversation that still is one I can say changed my life. It was simple. I was feeling sorry for myself and did not believe in myself. It wasn't what was said that helped, but the belief he still had in me. "Come on, get over yourself, and let's do some deals," is about how the conversation went. Great Dad advice.

It wasn't the words he gave me, it was the belief he was letting me borrow that changed me. I cannot stress the following statement enough if you cannot believe in yourself, right now.

So, with that said, borrow from this chapter. Borrow the belief. Believe me, if some kid from Carnes, Mississippi can find a way to make a happy life, anyone can.

Fast forward a few short years. Not only have we been able to build a successful real estate business, but we also built a platform, which has helped hundreds of people better their lives just like my father did for me. It's proven itself time and time again. I've become an authority figure, or leader, in my line of work. The strange lesson for me was that I still don't think of myself with those adjectives. I still think of myself as the guy who watched his life turn into a crater. And many of your most successful people in the world — despite amazing achievements financially, philanthropically, socially, and achieving fame — still see the person who may have failed, lost belief, or threw in the towel. But, the difference is, someone showed belief in them. Maybe a mentor, teacher, coach, sibling, parent, a book, a movie, or an educational course started them believing in themselves. Once the flame of belief is lit, we must take action and feed it.

We begin with teaching to believe in yourself. It's the biggest obstacle people have to overcome. Yes, you can make a living on your own. Yes, you can cold call a person and negotiate a deal. Yes, you can achieve a life outside the nine to five grind. It all begins with belief. Even though some newcomers may not have it, we are so confident in our process and have seen it work — we give them enough belief to begin taking action.

You see, dad lent me enough belief for me to take action, but the doing was up to me. It wasn't easy, but I put all my efforts and focus on helping others with their problems relative to my area of expertise — real estate. I literally stopped feeling sorry for myself and went to work helping others. At first, it was just distressed homeowners.

One homeowner, in particular, stands out. It helped lift the fog that had grown around my belief mechanism and I began to see a new path ahead...

A gentleman contacted me at 10 pm on a Tuesday night asking if I could help him. His house was being foreclosed on at 11 am Thursday — 37 hours from when the clock started.

Whew! This was going to be close. Not only was there an impending foreclosure, but his ex-wife was still on the deed and lived in another state. He had an active bankruptcy, two mortgages, and a judgment rendered after the bankruptcy. Exactly one hour before the forced sale, his life took a dramatic change. With his help, we were able to get his ex-wife to sign a deed, get title work done, prepare closing docs, discharge his bankruptcy, pay off the first and second mortgage, settle an HOA lien, and give him $1,000. It was a life-altering deal — even for me.

This specific deal reminded me that I had value, and so much more. I had value, because of what I could provide. It was my service that had value. I looked back over the previous 36 hours of whirlwind events. Boom! Epiphany time — I hadn't thought about my own problems the entire time. Not once! I focused on solving someone else's problems, that's it. By doing so, I was starting to solve my own problems by default.

In addition to belief, a servant mindset will change your life. When I began focusing on others is when I began to see the biggest changes in me. Zig Ziglar truly said it best, "You can have everything in life you want if you help enough people get what they want."

There are really not many problems that can't be solved with the right amount of help. I grew from a deal every few weeks to several a month, many times finding people in tough situations and with no help. In many cases, I was the only help they had. Knowing how I felt at my lowest, I know what people are going through in many of these situations.

It wasn't long before I came to the realization that I could show others how to do what I did. That's when the real fun ensued. In the summer of 2018, my good friend, and current business partner, Brent Moreno, had moved back to Mississippi. Together, we began teaching others how to help themselves by helping others. We started pumping out free content, hosting live events, and running small mastermind groups through our Real Estate Roundup Facebook group and Wholesale Hackers education platform. Today, our platforms reach thousands of people, and many of those now mentor other beginners. We grew by helping others grow. Steadily, our circle grew and what we were teaching people was working, before long not only did we have a circle of friends, we had a circle of influence. Now if a student comes to us with a problem, we have a network of helpers. Because those who are helping remember what it was like to need it themselves, that's how you keep the flame of belief lit — put good into the world and watch it succeed.

Our two mottos are "we're helpers, not hagglers" and "everything works if you do." We conduct business with that mindset. Again, you can have everything in life you want if you help enough people get what they want and do a bit of work.

When you approach life from the standpoint of service, watch your circle grow. When I was flying solo, I was flying high. But, when I crashed and burned, I was left watching a smoldering crater — alone. As I grew, my circle grew, and the opportunities did as well. It was through working with and helping others that I really saw myself grow into the person I wanted to be.

All of us have a powerful self — the one we always daydream ourselves to be! Yes, this includes you. I can unequivocally say it is true. Here's the catch, you'll never fully realize the potential person when that is simply your goal.

The powerful you will not be commanded.

In Mississippi, we have a saying: "Money and deals are like dogs; they run when you chase them." You have to quit chasing the short term and live the long term, and that means helping others, listening to what people actually have to say, helping people network, teaching a newbie — the list is endless.

By believing in yourself or finding a mentor, friend, or relative that believes in you, taking action in your life and ultimately having the mindset of helping others both in and out of business, there is another more powerful *you* growing.

This powerful you only will show up in your life when not directly called upon. Mine only started showing himself to work on my problems when I consumed myself with the problems of others.

CHAPTER 5

The Book Inside You

Founder/CEO of College Loan Freedom

 https://www.linkedin.com/in/larry-morrison

 https://www.facebook.com/collegeloanfreedom

 http://bit.ly/CLFVid

https://www.collegeloanfreedom.com/

Larry Morrison is one of America's leading experts on student loan debt repayment. He is a national speaker, a best-selling author, and founder of College Loan Freedom Inc. A company whose mission is to help borrowers navigate the complex government system meant to assist the millions who need help though less than 25% take advantage of. He regularly trains financial advisors on how to reallocate resources away from student debt to growing wealth for their clients. He also teaches at graduate schools all over the country to students ready to leave school and tackle their loans. His passion is helping student loan borrowers remove the fear and shame associated with the debt because in his words it is a "paper tiger" once you understand the system. His best selling book is *Student Loan Debt Secrets – An Insider Explains Why You Are Overpaying When Thousands Aren't* is available on Amazon.

If you are a financial professional who would like to learn more about helping your clients with the second-biggest debt in the United States or if you have a loved one who needs help managing their student loan debt reach out to Larry for assistance by emailing thestudentloanexpert@gmail.com or visiting CollegeLoanFreedom.com

*"There is no greater agony than bearing
an untold story inside you."*

— M AYA A NGELOU

I don't pretend to know what you believe about yourself or the universe you live in. However, I believe you can write your book, the book that is inside of you waiting to be born. Like a fingerprint, it will be uniquely your own. I'm not going to tell you how to write it because it would deprive you of the experience. I'm simply going to share how I wrote my own book with the intention that it might benefit you in the creation process, especially if you have never written a book before. Take what you like and leave what you don't.

When I was first inspired to write a book, I knew what I wanted to write, the subject about which I was an authority and completely enveloped in every day. Working in your subject gives plenty of inspirations that you want to put in your book. After I started writing, I would come across a situation and think, "Oh, I have to put that in the book." On the flip side, if you are not immersed in your subject daily, it can be a blessing, because the last thing you want to do is to come home and write about it. Either way, wherever you are is the perfect place to begin.

No matter which subject you choose, adopt the idea that It wants to be written about, that It has chosen to come through you using your words, your perception, and your voice. Even though there might be a thousand other books on the subject, your authentic voice is what It craves. No one can duplicate your brush strokes or experiences. We never say to an artist, "You know what, I think the world has enough paintings of ocean sunsets." Or, "We don't need any more pictures of children laughing." This is the perfect time to add your take on the story.

BRAIN DUMP

When I first began writing, something I had never done before, I didn't know where to begin. Should I create an outline and begin with Chapter One? Maybe I should research how the best writers begin attacking the blank page. I decided I didn't care about how others had done it; I just wanted to write. I adopted the notion that if the book needed massive editing, it could be done after I said what I wanted to say.

Once the inspiration struck me, It wouldn't let go, although it was six months from when the idea came to me that I started to write, and another several months before the book got dedicated time on my calendar. The more time I gave to It, the more It took on a life of its own, and It would nag at me every day until completion. It created a feeling inside of me, wanting to be freed. So, when I finally listened, I opened the flood gates and didn't attempt to control what came out.

In business, when approaching a problem, it is helpful to do a brain dump. The act of letting all the ideas flow surrounding the issue in whatever random form they pop into your brain and writing it all down. Once you are sure it's all out, you can look at it on paper and begin to prioritize the challenges, ideas, and solutions into the next steps. That is what I did with the book. I just started writing and writing with no structure, but an extremely loose outline — Part One: The problem and how we got here (past). Part Two: The solutions I used daily to fix the problem (present). Part Three: How we can correct the problem going forward (future). When writing, I would look at the tense of what was pouring out and slot it under these three categories with no influence on what I had previously written or what came next. It was just a way to keep my ramblings filed, knowing

I would come back and organize it later. My heart wanted to just write wild and free. I didn't want to do anything to hinder that flow, like worrying about organizational structure.

I'm not saying you should write this way, only that you need to become aware of what gets you into that flow state where the words come pouring out, and you lose all sense of time and space, plus anything that stops the flow. Then, writing takes on a life of its own, and it becomes less of a chore to do. When I was inspired, I would write. When I wasn't, I would block time to be inspired, but if nothing came, I would organize what was written — fixing typos, grammar, and sentence placement. There were times when life took over and writing would go back to a nagging sensation. Then there were days I would wake up with tons of ideas and writing got in the way of life. I rescheduled meetings, missed social events, and gym time, because inspiration had grabbed hold of me, and I happily gave into it.

Once I wrote like this for quite some time, I began to see these giant chunks of writing as wet clay that needed to be molded into place. When I would organize the words, I could see where there were gaps that needed to be filled. Those gaps had inherent inspiration because they needed bridges, sentences, paragraphs, or whole pages that would neatly tie two concepts together. This is how an idea that transformed into a nagging sensation began to take shape into a book. However, I was not immune to becoming overwhelmed.

COMPARISON TRAP

You see, my subject matter is extremely complex, and the book had to tackle these complexities in a no-nonsense way. However, it meant that I was going to have to write a lot. There were so many times after I had written my heart out that I would look at the scope of it and say to myself, "There is so much more that needs to be discussed." I would then get discouraged and think, "maybe I shouldn't be this detailed about each step," therefore shortchanging myself, the book, and the reader. I fell into the trap of looking how far I had to go up the mountain instead of how far I had come.

This is when I learned to let go. Not let go of writing, but let go of the arbitrary deadlines for finishing that I had imagined. The truth is, I had never written a book before, so how would I know how long it should take? I had to surrender to the love of writing itself — the love of being in the flow state and watching what comes from it. I gave up thinking about Its completion and wrote for the love of the subject and the purpose It had given me. This book needed to be birthed, but not half-assed.

Then it was time to sculpt. For me, the fun part was re-reading what I had written to determine how to say it better. I love reading it through the eyes of someone else. How are they going to hear it in their mind, how am I presenting the information, how do the chapters flow together, and build on top of one another? Are there any facts the reader needs before proceeding to the next? But, best of all, does it grab and keep their attention?

While sculpting, I'm also on a mission to condense the book. To find redundancies, to strip away the fluff, and tightly weave concepts together. Do I really need this paragraph, is it crucial, does it move things along in the right direction? If it is necessary, can I say it in one or two sentences instead of five? This is where a quality team can be crucial.

RESEARCH

When most of it was out of me and on paper, then it was time for research. I wanted my book to be bulletproof, which meant backing up all the facts with hard data. At first, researching facts to support my arguments was uncomfortable and didn't feel like the writing flowed anymore. Then I resisted data that didn't support my arguments, thinking, "I don't trust their study on the subject. All numbers can be manipulated to fit their point of view." It dawned on me that I was accusing others of doing what I was attempting to do. Have the numbers fit my argument instead of me adapting to them.

It was time to bring an unbiased perspective, so I hired a researcher to source all the claims I had made as "fact." Most were correct, but some were not. I shored up the weak points by changing my hypotheses to fit the data instead of forcing my views on certain aspects that had been revealed to me as incorrect. Research is your friend, and while you are undoubtedly an authority about the subject on which you are writing, the data only makes you better when having your theories tested by others. An opinion is easy to ignore, but facts are not.

INTENTION

With writing, you must always adhere to the intention of your book. I like to let the reader know the intention right in the beginning, so it binds you both to it. The intention will guide you in the editing process as well when it comes to what constructive criticisms to keep, what changes to make, and what inputs to ignore. If your intention with the book is to help people, maybe help them avoid a mistake, or tackle some problem, then ask yourself if the edit helps accomplish that. Be aware that your ego can get in the way by holding onto things that don't serve the intention. If there is an edit, you don't want to make ask yourself, "Will it help more people or add more value?"

In the end, when the book was completed, I sat down with my publisher. I had written 180,000 words. My publisher said, "Oh my gosh, you wrote three books, no wonder it took you so long." I had no idea that the average book was 55,000 – 65,000 words because I didn't care what anyone else was doing. I was letting the book come through me. We settled on splitting the manuscript up into two 90,000-word books. Which was a great compromise, because people can read Book One, which is Part One and Two (past and present), to get the help they need. Then, Part Three addresses how we can correct the problem going forward and is not essential to help struggling people. So, *Student Loan Debt Secrets – An Insider Explains Why You Are Overpaying When Thousands Aren't* was officially born.

FINAL THOUGHTS

Your expertise on the subject will shine through the pages if given to the reader in a usable way. Be careful about tooting your own horn versus using your experience with the subject to move the book along.

When it comes to structuring, start simple and build on it, getting more complex as you go. When you have gone deep into a complex aspect, use examples of how it works in real life to bring the complexity down to the tangible.

You may believe you are not a writer or even an authority. But, I know there is a book inside you begging to come out. The real work is to find your unique way to be a conduit for It to come through you.

Make a mess, be sloppy, screw it up, who cares since it is yours, and no one will see it until you are ready. Let go of structure, self-judgment, and perfectionism. Doubt any voice that stops the flow and robs us of your masterpiece.

"Don't Die With Your Music Still Inside You"

– WAYNE DYER

Good journey, my friends.

CHAPTER 6

Writing as a Reinvention Strategy: How I Wrote a Book and Launched My New Business (and how you can, too)!

Cathy Fyock,

CSP, SPHR, SHRM-SCP

The Business Book Strategist

 https://www.linkedin.com/in/cathy-fyock-973b735/

 https://www.facebook.com/TheBusinessBookStrategist/

 https://twitter.com/CathyFyock

 https://www.cathyfyock.com/

Cathy Fyock, CSP, is The Business Book Strategist and works with thought leaders and professionals who want to grow their businesses by writing a book. She is the author of — On Your Mark: From First Word to First Draft in Six Weeks, Blog2Book: Repurposing Content to Discover the Book You've Already Written, and her most recent, The Speaker Author: Sell More Books and Book More Business. Since starting her book coaching business in 2014, she's helped more than 180 professionals become published authors.

Cathy's book coaching practice includes one-on-one coaching, three-day writing retreats, writing workshop, forums, and group coaching, in addition to speaking for thought leaders at conferences and chapter meetings.

Have you ever been in that place where you knew you needed to make a career change? I was at this juncture in 2013 when working for a consulting firm: I missed the autonomy of having my own business; I wanted to spend less time on the road; I needed a change.

As I look back, it's amazing to me that by writing a book I could completely change the trajectory of my career and become happier and more fulfilled than I had in any other job. But then, that's the magic of authoring a book — it gives you that authority.

I got the idea for this new business direction when I received a call from the president of my chapter of the National Speakers Association. He said he'd heard a rumor that I had written one of my books in less than six weeks.

"Actually, I've written four of my five books in less than six weeks," I told him at that time.

Then he asked me one of the most important questions of my life. "Do you have a *process?*"

I thought for a moment, and I said, "Yes, I do."

Next, he asked if I would be willing to present a class on my process at an upcoming chapter meeting, and I jumped at the suggestion. He then said, "But wait, before you say yes, we have two members of our chapter who are writing their own books. Would you be willing to coach them using your process and then provide a program based on your experience?"

I accepted his challenge wholeheartedly. After all, if the process worked for me, why wouldn't it work for others?

A few weeks into the coaching process these two women said to me, "Have you ever thought about becoming a book coach?"

'A book coach? Is there such a thing? Is there a need?'

They assured me that there were many individuals who wanted to establish their authority. Speakers, consultants, coaches, and other entrepreneurs who derived business from their expertise — who wanted and even needed to write a book, and were among those who were unsure how to begin or how to reach the finish line.

I initially dismissed the idea; however, after presenting my chapter program, my friends came to me and asked, "Have you ever thought about being a book coach?"

Now the idea was beginning to sink in.

I began putting my business plan together for my book coaching practice and developing my exit strategy from my current role.

How can I establish myself as an authority on writing books? The answer came to me loud and clear: I needed to write a book about how to write a book! And, if my process is about how to write a book in six weeks, I need to write this book in six weeks.

Yes, I had written books before in my field of human resource management that established my expertise as an HR consultant, but now I needed to write this new book about my process of writing non-fiction books quickly and efficiently.

Six years later, I've helped more than 180 professionals become published authors, and finished several new books on writing as well.

What if you want to reinvent yourself? I believe that you, too, can make this shift through authorship.

First, establish the expertise where you'd like to focus. Ideally, pick something for which you have a passion, as well as expertise. When I began as a book coach, I already had the background of writing five books which grew my previous business. While I never enjoyed writing (I think that it's hard work!), I absolutely loved the benefits of having written. I adore the prestige of having written a book. I love owning the space of thought leadership around a topic. I enjoy being "the one who wrote the book on it."

In my case, I needed to determine the steps involved in my book-writing process. For example, I knew that it was important to create the purpose for your book, which in my case was to serve as a calling card for my coaching practice and the curriculum for my training and workshops. I also needed to create a strategic plan for my book that aligned with my new business's strategy.

Consider this for your business:

- Do you offer a unique framework, a creative lens, or a new perspective for solving problems?
- Do you create new models, processes, or systems for a unique approach to an issue?
- Do you use your own terminology or create new terms to define new concepts and become quotable?
- Do you brand your ideas and concepts or present them in new and unique ways?

Codify your thought leadership. Writing is an amazing way to gain clarity about your process or ideas. By writing each chapter as a part of the strategy, I found that I was clarifying in my own mind the steps that I would use to lead my clients in writing their nonfiction books.

Some additional ideas:

- Don't merely repackage the knowledge of other thought leaders; build on their ideas. Read extensively from a variety of business and professional journals. Know how your ideas are similar to those of others, as well as how and why you offer a unique view.

- Create your own model, process, or system by using powerful analogies and metaphors to define concepts that are part of your brand.

- Don't quote others; quote yourself. Create sound bites that are sticky.

I had the benefit of providing coaching to two Beta clients who weren't paying for my services. This allowed me to see if my process worked, and how it might need to be modified to benefit others. I have changed my coaching process over time, based on my experience in working with a variety of clients on a wide spectrum of topics.

Write your book. Now comes the hard part — actually sitting down and documenting your thought leadership. What are the steps you must take? What expertise must you already possess? What will your reader need to know that you already have learned?

You must also demonstrate your expertise throughout your book. You do this by telling stories about your experience with your topic and through client stories about how they've used your principles or process to complete their hero's journey.

I could write an entire book about how to write a book (and I have with my book, On Your Mark: From First Word to First Draft in Six Weeks), but some key points include:

Put the writing time on your calendar and not on your "to-do" list since we typically work our task list by what is urgent. While your book is important, it likely never will be urgent.

Set a goal for completing the book, and create benchmarks for your project plan. If you want to write a book in six weeks as I have, and your book has six chapters, the simple math says that you must write at least one chapter each week!

Don't edit until you've written your first draft. We know from brain science that creative writing and editing are two distinct brain functions. When you edit while you write you likely feel exhausted because your brain has been working double time!

If you can't seem to make the time or have the focus you need, you may want to enlist the support of a book coach. Be sure to select someone who has expertise within your genre. For example, my forte is helping thought leaders write a nonfiction book that supports their business growth.

Overcome self-limiting beliefs. One of the most difficult aspects of stepping into a new field and changing your direction — and writing your book — is the negative voice that lives inside your head. This is the voice that says, *'Whoever said that you could write?' 'Don't you think someone else is better qualified to write this book?' 'Aren't there enough books on your topic already?' 'Who's going to buy your book?'*

There is something about overcoming these personal demons as you write the book that allows you to fully step into your authority once you're an author. You master the "imposter syndrome" and understand that you own the right to claim this expertise as an authority and thought leader.

Promote your book and your new business. Just writing the book doesn't mean that your book will magically create business opportunities. You must now wield your book — your magic wand — to unlock its magic.

In my most recent book, *The Speaker Author: Sell More Books and Book More Speeches*, coauthor Lois Creamer and I, outline key ideas for how to leverage your book to sell more books, book more speeches, and develop new business opportunities. I'm identifying several ideas here:

1. Identify yourself as an author! Include the book cover on your email signature (Author of the book . . .), your website, and other personal marketing assets.

2. Speak for conferences and programs as "The Author of . . ." and use the book's title as your keynote's title.

3. When you speak, reference your book during your presentation. We've also found that by holding the book and reading from it, you create additional interest in sales following the talk.

4. Negotiate with meeting planners to include books as part of your package when speaking.

5. Give away select books to key stakeholders to generate interest and to link your name with your topic.

6. Create media opportunities with the new book to generate interest in your new business.

West Point graduate, Sara Potecha, wanted to speak on leadership and provide consulting in the leadership space. While she had other credentials, her book, *West Point Woman*, gave her much added power and punch in this space. Her now lucrative speaking and consulting business is in part due to her authority on this topic through authorship.

Another client, Karl Richter, had similar success by writing a chapter in an anthology set (much like this one). His chapter in *You@Work* featured his work as a thought leader in online and blended learning. He also has attributed several pieces of six-figure work to his connection with the book.

Client, Eric Williamson, was reinventing his career as a speaker, trainer, and consultant, when he wrote his book, *How to Work with*

Jerks, as a strategy to jump-start his business. Similarly, retired United States Army Colonel Rob Campbell wrote his book, *It's Personal (Not Personnel)*, when establishing his reinvention as a leadership speaker, trainer, and consultant.

Sometimes authorship can springboard more than just a career; it can birth a movement or a ministry. Client Laurie Hellmann wrote, *Welcome to My Life: A Personal Parenting Journey through Autism*, to position her work in advocacy for families dealing with autism and to launch her new podcast on that subject. Sarah Hellmann, Ph.D., is an author, artist, and speaker. She founded the ministry Art for All People to inspire others to use their inherent creativity toward healing and empowerment in her book, *Broken-Down Jalopies and other Short Stories (Perspective Changes Everything)*.

And, what have I personally gained through authorship and reinvention? I'm working as an entrepreneur — in charge of my business and my life. I'm happier and more fulfilled in my work than I've ever been since I believe that I am doing holy work in helping others step into their potential — their authority.

So, what would you like to be when you grow up? Are you ready to reinvent yourself?

Perhaps a book will be just the tool you need to springboard to your next endeavor. Unlike any other credential, it will say to others that "you wrote the book on it!"

CHAPTER 7

Gaining Your Voice of Authority: Recognizing, respecting, and connecting with your audience — personally and professionally

Allan McLennan

p.g.a.

Chief Executive, PADEM Media Group/USA, Global Streaming Media Market Developer, Technologist & Analyst

 https://www.linkedin.com/in/allannmclennan/

 www.pademmediagroup.com/books

Allan McLennan is a streaming media expert, entrepreneur, commentator, and adviser to digital media companies. He is the founder, Chief Executive, and lead analyst of the San Francisco based PADEM Media Group, a media technology, market advancement consulting firm.

Allan's 25+ year dedication to the global streaming media, data intelligent/AI, and connected device revolution as a C-suite senior market growth executive has enabled him to contribute to and work with extraordinary companies, inventors, scientists, technologists, accomplished executives, and high performing companies such as Ericsson; Siemens; Microsoft; Spielberg; APPLE and Disney.

With numerous global firsts he has developed/deployed products/services on five continents/17 countries to hundreds of millions of households and screens, from the first global streaming IP/OTT offering; founding president of US publicly traded data analytics firm RENTRAK to today advancing new education streaming services and category M&A.

Allan is active in the Academy of Television Arts and Sciences (EMMY's); Producers Guild of America; Society of Motion Pictures Television Engineers; Board Director for IET/London and CEI (Center of Educational Innovation - NYC); Advisory Board for RightsTrade/LA (film/television licensing marketplace); an MBA International Strategy (team/behavioural economics); global speaker on media ecology and is a guest lecturer at Stanford Graduate School of Business.

H aving an authoritative voice is one of the most important assets a business or person can have in today's world. Being recognized by your audience as a trustworthy thought leader is critically important and something for which every person and company should strive.

If you already have this capability, then you are a lucky person. You have had an aha moment when asked for your opinion and then realized that you have what it takes to provide an overall connection to that audience. Your experience, insights, and credentials you brought to the conversation caused you to be recognized as an authority.

It takes time and effort to arrive at this moment. Especially effort. Time, on the other hand, is relative. For more than 40 years, I have been on a journey to connect audiences through media and in those connections, with societies and their cultures around the world. Whether it was my being a radio talk show host, movie production gopher, television show/series producer, magazine publisher, advertising market strategist, software developer, digital content creator, virtual avatar, streaming service enabler, president of a publicly-traded company, technology innovator, entrepreneur, buyer and seller of companies, corporate growth accelerator, and corporate C-suite executive, I have focused on understanding and studying how company teams and event audiences responded to what was being said and then the impact that our products had through the media we produced. The list of projects, products, technologies, and companies is long and could come off as possibly being perceived as bravado, but it is not. Each engagement, experience, failure, and success has helped provide valuable and applicable disciplines, insight, and a bit of wisdom to further a journey and refinement of credentials and to create a depth of authority.

Over time you can hit upon a great idea or capitalize on a need, but it takes true instinct, knowledge, and intelligence to look beyond where you are at that moment to identify trends, study them, and then pursue a path of evolutionary and intellectual discovery to build new expertise. This process alone can have a tremendous impact on your belief in yourself, which in turn drives your journey. Authority doesn't just magically appear, it takes effort, failure, persistence, and success to bring to the table actual insight that will establish your authority. Your personality, confidence, and especially your respect for your audience will take over in crafting your engagements.

Realizing that you've started down this path and gained your audience's respect truly is rewarding. In my case, this came from years of exploration, working to build credentials in digital distribution technology, media, streaming entertainment, virtual education, publishing, and data intelligence. Curiously, this wasn't part of my initial plan. I wanted to be a film director. So, I started out producing a radio talk show when I was in high school, kids show in college, community service campaign for the handicapped, and then, to make money, strung coax for a new cable company while in college. Surprisingly, my comfort in standing in front of an audience launched me in being able to help manage and communicate. This ability led me to advertising, film, and television management, the creation and publishing of multiple magazines, production of television programs, and development of entertainment technical platforms, which became the thread throughout my experience, building a depth of understanding, learning to listen to individuals who knew more than I did, and applying wisdom when identifying new challenges. This helped me identify needs, solve issues and problems in product innovation, engagement, and growth. Understanding how these puzzle pieces fit together and the ability to accurately deliver clarity and actionable solutions became my vehicle to honestly connect with audiences around the world.

When stepping up and engaging an audience, there are a few things you need to understand; the first is why your audience is there and what they are looking for from you. Being able to respond quickly and accurately to their expectation will be key to engaging them. It almost goes without saying that you need to focus on your area of expertise. This is why, for example, a health professional might have difficulty in addressing a unified software issue for efficient video delivery. Your likelihood of being perceived as an authority depends on your actual expertise, but also your understanding of your audience. This is especially true in the media and entertainment world, where the reputation of an authoritative person can be just as important as their actual skills in establishing trust.

Presenting yourself accurately and honestly is a strategic process. Work to position yourself as someone who has been in your audience's shoes, then demonstrate how you have developed a process that successfully navigates the challenges that they currently are facing. It is in this exchange that you begin to be perceived as an expert, especially if you create a specific plan, recognize, and respect your audience's needs, and then share your insights to intelligently connect. This is especially true in today's virtualized and digitalized world when many times we are engaging virtually.

When connecting virtually, it is key to be authentic. This can be accomplished by sharing the challenges you've faced and told your audience about the insights you gained through failures, as well as successes, and the expertise you have learned along the way. When your audience is able to identify, recognize, and establish your credibility, they can make a case as to why you are the best resource for them. When you do not feel the need to sell whatever you're proposing, then you have arrived.

For example, when I have worked to identify market shifts and societal trends, I have tried to carefully explain key differentiations in order to present what I have discovered. If I am not careful and use incorrect words, my message can be (and has been) easily misunderstood and misconstrued. If this happens, there is a good chance that you will miss an opportunity to communicate your insights as every word has its place. The need to be accurate and provide rational reasons is never greater than during this time.

The explosion of digital connections for so many people throughout the world now provides even more opportunities for you to become recognized as an expert. Traditionally, writing and publishing a book was enough to establish one as an authority, and interestingly enough, it still is. A book can be consumed in old-school paper format, it can be downloaded to devices instantaneously throughout the world, and also can be consumed in audio format. In years past we mostly engaged face-to-face, but today, your content and message can be created and distributed by podcast, blog posts, articles, video, and many more choices on so many different platforms that the path for you to become a recognized authority is greater than ever.

So, how do you become someone who stands out as an authority instead of remaining unknown? Is it your appearance, or is it identifying the problem and focusing on solving it, quickly? Then it is identifying an audience that needs this expertise and presenting yourself as a trustworthy individual with a valuable solution.

When you are interacting as a trustworthy person with your audience, it can become easy to confuse your influence and passion with authority if you are not careful. Many speakers who carry the mantle of "authority" believe that they know the differences, but most do not and this is another critically important point. If you are blessed with authority, it is important for your long-term success to provide honest answers and manage your authoritative presence. This is true whether you're an evangelist who is in front of a congregation, an influential news anchor, as well as a business or political leader. Being in that position, your audiences can be manipulated by passionate messages, and those messages can potentially do harm to your audience well into the future.

One of the most valuable skills is to be clear and insightful when in front of a group. This skill can enable you to be looked upon as a thought leader in your field, whether you are a dentist, doctor, mathematician, salesperson, baseball, or foosball player. When you master this skill, you can rise to the top of your game, systematically engaging your audience, and enabling you to strategically deliver a strong message.

This is especially true when interacting through digital media and streaming television. When you are dedicated to serving your audience, providing helpful information and opinion becomes incredibly valuable in retaining your viewers and helping increase your authority. Your expertise that enables you to connect with large audiences is key in our current digital environment, too. Just as in face-to-face engagements, it is especially important to make a strong first impression, but it is complicated in the digital world because your audience is going to be researching you online. Therefore, you need to nurture your digital image and message. Implementing the four pillars of connecting with your audience and enhancing your authority is to plan, understand, respect, and share.

For example, planning enables you to be concise and clear. Without planning, you can quickly get lost in what you're going to say. Understanding your audience enables you to appear organized and sharp. Without understanding with whom you are engaging, runs the risk of being perceived as unprepared, even if you are a known subject matter expert. Respecting your audience and the challenges they face makes you seem interesting and engaged. If you don't respect your audience's needs and just focus on what you want to tell them, you will likely lose their attention and be hard-pressed to share your insights, skills, and connect intelligently.

Why is this important? Early in my career, we were working on a new software platform that associated decisions the users made to how they learned. Structurally, this enabled an accelerated decision tree that served up informed responses, so that a person could be identifying how they embraced and retained information. This connectivity led to building some of the first and most successful educational, interactive storybooks and helped enable some of the first steps in digital engagement. When we launched Lion King, we created the first interactive storybooks for children, followed by Little Mermaid, 101 Dalmatians, and more. Having an understanding of how our audience accepted and retained information was a driving factor that helped us build valuable and authoritative products.

Years later, this ability to understand how our audience absorbed information is especially important in this time of COVID-19. It is critical that true experts communicate clearly and truthfully while understanding and respecting their audiences. Lives depend upon it. We are witnessing that connecting with audiences and delivering influential messages requires clear, honest communications, and a deep understanding of, as well as respect for the audience. If not, the authority will wither away.

Almost everyone has the drive, passion, and ability to succeed at a given task if they are focused and clear on what they've learned and can accurately represent their knowledge. When this engagement occurs, we have the opportunity to create better products and build communities that help audiences evolve through sharing in-depth analysis from focused research, intelligent data, inventive conclusions, and historical facts.

For four decades I have had the opportunity to participate in the amazing growth and development of media technology, which has taught me the critical importance of how being an authentic expert who connects respectfully with an audience can help influence culture worldwide. I encourage you to venture out and connect with your voice of authority!

CHAPTER 8

How to Build Your Reputation and Become the Authority

Jenn Foster

15X Bestselling Author

 https://www.linkedin.com/in/jennfosterseo

 https://www.facebook.com/authorjennfoster/

 https://www.instagram.com/jennfosterchic

 https://authorjennfoster.com/

Jenn Foster is a fifteen-times bestselling author, one of today's national leading digital marketing specialists, an award-winning web designer, and recipient of the esteemed "Quilly Award". She is the Founder/Owner of Elite Online Publishing as well as Founder/CEO of Biz Social Boom.

She is dedicated to helping businesses use powerful new online and mobile marketing platforms to get visibility, traffic, leads, customers, and raving fans. She is passionate about helping busy entrepreneurs, business leaders, and professionals to create, publish, and market their book, to build their business and brand. She encourages new authors to share their stories, knowledge, and expertise to help others and leave a legacy to the world.

Jenn is a graduate of Utah State University. She owned and operated a chain of successful retail stores. Jenn has been named one of America's Premier Experts® and is highlighted in the Dan Kennedy Book, Stand Apart. She was recently named one of "Utah's Thought Leaders" in the book Innovate Utah by Global Village. Jenn is the co-host of Elite Expert Insider Podcast on iTunes and Libsyn Radio. Jenn is a single mother, loves spending time with her three children and experiencing the great outdoors.

YOU MAY KNOW YOU ARE AN EXPERT, BUT DOES ANYONE ELSE KNOW?

I recently spoke with a man who served in two presidential administrations in international affairs. He traveled the globe representing our country and had a resume that read like a textbook. Sadly, he currently is unemployed, over 50 years old, and has no idea how to reposition himself in his market. This happens to countless individuals. They have a wealth of knowledge, but no one outside their circle knows who they are, the knowledge they possess, and the authority they bring.

How can he literally rewrite his future and his story? You can't do this by just having a LinkedIn profile.

The smartest thing you can do to reposition yourself as an expert, and industry leader, is **build a platform of raving fans**. One of the best and easiest ways to be known as an authority, attract new job offers, **buyers, clients, and fans** is through a **podcast and a book**. Watch your business grow as you create unique, expert content. By either having your own podcast or being a guest on a podcast, you'll expand your reach through your audience, connect with podcasters, put the word out about you, as well as your business, and build trust.

The question is... What exactly is my expertise again?

Most of our clients are multifaceted and don't know what they should choose as their one topic to write or talk about.

What is the best thing that will set them apart as the authority? This is where most people get stuck, so they end up doing nothing. They just keep spinning ideas on the hamster wheel in their head. They feel like they have so many different directions and ideas that they just can't choose. Not choosing is a choice that gets you nowhere.

To help our authors get over this hurdle, we host what's called a **VIP Book or Podcast Creation Day**. This gives our clients clarity, purpose, and direction. We spend a whole day with our clients crafting their message and creating a complete detailed outline for their book or podcast. During the VIP day, the most important question we ask is, "What is the end result you are seeking?"

If you have several different career options we suggest you write them all down. Rate them from one to 10 (with 10 being the highest) of which ones you enjoy doing the most and which ones are the most profitable. Start with the one that ranks the highest for profitability and enjoyment. That's the best place to start. It takes the same amount of energy to pursue or create something that makes you $1 million dollars as it does $10,000. Your time is your time and once it's gone you can never get it back.

To help you find your authority here is a little taste of what we do for our **VIP Book or Podcast Creation Day** clients.

The first thing we start with is **YOU**.

BOOST YOUR CONFIDENCE AND SELF ESTEEM

Focus on your successes, not your failures, then make a list of your successes. Try the mirror test — before you go to bed, stand in front of the mirror, and tell yourself what you appreciate about yourself and acknowledge your value for that day. For example:

- "I passed up that piece of cake today"
- "I wrote three chapters in my book today"

1. Let's Brainstorm Your Personal Story or Narrative! Consider how people describe your business...

- For what do you want to be known?
- What is the ideal or core promise that you represent in your marketplace?
- What is it your readers aspire to have, do, share, or be, that you can reflect back to them?

2. Define You

- Pick your passion!
- What is your superpower (personally or in business)?
- What would be your core promise to the marketplace?
- What are they saying about you and your brand?
- What role can your business/expertise play in their lives?
- What are your clients' wants and needs in your area of expertise?

3. What are some of your biggest problems or pain points that you have with engaging your target market?

- Problem or pain #3?
- Problem or pain #2?
- Problem or pain #1?

4. What are the primary objections or concerns potential readers may have about engaging with you and ultimately doing business with you?

- What is their first objection or concern working with you?
- What is the solution to their first objection or concern working with you?
- What is their second objection or concern working with you?
- What is the solution to their second objection or concern working with you?
- What is their third objection or concern working with you?
- What is the solution to their third objection or concern working with you?

5. BRAINSTORM — In two sentences describe:

- How is your product or service different from others?
- What message do you want to give your target market? (Nike Just Do It)
- What inspired you to get into your career? Was it a mentor? Friend?
- Pros and Cons of your topic. Dos and Don'ts.
- FAQ's.

Summary and Homework

- Describe your business and what you want to be known for
- Define you, your passion, and your superpower
- Your market's biggest pain points
- The primary objections or concerns of your readers and clients
- Brainstorm and write down several life experience stories of yours or others. You can use just one or two words if you want to prompt you to the story
- What makes your product or service different from others. Pros and Cons/Dos and Don'ts.
- Remember to be real, genuine, and in a great mindset when writing all this down. This is the start of the road for your book.

> *"If you can't explain it to a six-year-old, you don't know it yourself."*
>
> — ALBERT EINSTEIN

Now that you know what your message is you can start using it. How do you get your foot in the door and make an impression on the CEO or company by whom you are trying to get hired? Invite them to be a guest on your podcast! Yes, that's right! You can pick people you want to interview, who you want as your clients, to be on your show. It's a great way to get in front of the clients, bosses, or customers you've been trying to reach. The key is, you're offering value to them by interviewing them on your show. We've secured quite a few clients just from being a guest on our show. We bought products from our guests and have started successful collaborations from our podcast interviews. We have even repurposed the content from our podcast and created two bestselling books from it: ***Podcast Authorized: Turn***

Your Podcast Into a Book That Builds Your Business and *Book Writing Bible: Expert Secrets on How to Write, Sell, & Market Your Book Online.*

More than 50% of the homes are podcast fans! Podcasts are poised to eclipse traditional radio in listenership, and **podcasts are opening the door** to individuals, businesses, and celebrities alike, to have their own show, with no barrier to entry.

When you create a podcast or are a guest on a podcast, it's extremely helpful to have a book to go with it. Then you have content, and people can find you on Amazon to get more content from you afterward. You could even use your book as a give-away on your podcast. Whether you're on a podcast, or you have one of your own, you can give your book away as an added bonus. It provides trust for your audience, clients, and prospects. You are building your business and associations by having the book and having the interviews on podcasts as well.

Here is the link to our podcast *Elite Expert Insider:* Bit.ly/eliteexpertinsider.

Don't forget to SUBSCRIBE on iTunes and YouTube, so you never miss an episode.

YouTube is: https://youtu.be/hjXbRxLBpqQ.

For either your podcast or your book, remember a significant story is essential for entrepreneurs and business owners to tell and market their story. When you can share your story, you'll be a better leader. There's just one story that entrepreneurs must never forget to tell, as it's arguably the most important one for their business to succeed: their own personal story. It gives people a reason to believe in you and allows you to set yourself up as a leading authority and expert in your industry.

The power of a compelling, connected, well-crafted, and well-delivered story is that it short-circuits a lot of the things normally required to find and attract your ideal customers. Your book will target your ideal customer and set you up to work with the exact types of people you seek.

Even with all the advances in technology, the fastest way to deliver your message to your desired market is still through the power of a story. Your story creates an immediate connection, emotion, and desire in your target market to want to be part of the bigger picture of what you're about in life. It gives them hope that they can get past whatever is stopping them from achieving their biggest goals and dreams.

The following are 10 things we use to help Elite Online Publishing Authors tell their story.

Fast Track Thought Starter:

1. Your life before you?
2. How did you realize you needed to make a change?
3. Why you did it?
4. When and how did you do it?
5. Specific ways it has changed your life.
6. Tips — I used to think, now I think.
7. Think through your story.
   - How does it demonstrate your points?
8. Ways to begin your story.
   - I used to think, I used to be afraid, or I didn't understand, now I understand.

9. Ways to end your story.

- Grateful.

- Close with questions.

- Where do you still want to grow?

10. BE VULNERABLE.

There is no better way to build your reputation as an influencer than becoming an authority with a podcast and a book. Stand out from the competition and position yourself as a thought leader. Unlock career opportunities that you never would have imagined. Reach levels of success you wouldn't necessarily reach otherwise.

Back in 2013, I wrote my first book. Actually it was a chapter in a book, *Stand Apart: Stand Out Strategies from Today's Leading Entrepreneurs and Professionals to Help You Achieve Health, Wealth, and Success*, with Dan Kennedy. My chapter transformed my marketing company. Once the book hit the shelves on Amazon, my phone kept ringing and didn't stop. I had people calling me to ask me to white label my marketing services. A man from Boise, ID, called and left a voicemail.

"It's three o'clock in the morning and I've read your chapter over and over again. I own a marketing company, and I've realized I'm missing a ton of things. Can you serve my clients? Do you have a discounted price or a white label service?"

I got so many calls, it filled up my client list within two weeks of the book being released. I told my story in my chapter, as well as taught valuable marketing skills for online local sales, as well as video marketing skills. After writing that chapter, I knew I had to write another book. As of today, I have written 15 books. All 15 of them have become #1 Bestsellers on Amazon. All of these books have helped me gain additional clients, as well as provide valuable content for them.

Now is the time. **Get out there! Create your podcast! Write your book!**

As our gift to help get you started, get our FREE BOOK *Accomplishment and Personal Success Story Starter* by texting your Name and Email to: (832) 572-5285.

CHAPTER 9

Your Authentic Self: Where Authority Lives

Denise Gabel

High Trust Environment – Author,
Speaker, and Professional Advisor.

 https://www.linkedin.com/in/denise-gabel-5010794/

 http://thedenise.com/

Denise is an author, speaker, and professional advisor. She works with executives and their teams to build high trust environments.

Through storytelling from the stage or by video, Denise encourages people to embrace change, stand in their own authentic power, and help organizations think big.

Denise is the former Chief Innovation Officer of the Filene Research Institute where she led the prestigious i3 innovation program throughout the U.S. and Canada. Denise served as Chief Operating Officer at the Northwest Credit Union Association where she helped re-invent what a regional trade association does. She and the team have bragging rights to the high trust environment they built – together.

Gabel is a summa cum laude graduate of Eastern Washington University and served as a member of the Berkeley Innovation Forum at the University of California Berkeley Haas School of Business. She also graduated from the Harvard Business School's Women's Leadership Forum.

As a change agent, Denise always has a new book underway. She is honored to have her soulmate serving in his chief angel capacity gently pushing her to reach her full potential. Always.

Spend time with Denise – it will change your life.

You *have* authority when you get a title. You *become* an authority when you stand in your own authentic power — when you harness and use your unique talents and gifts. When you *own* what you own.

Finding your authentic self — standing in your own authentic power — is a journey that uniquely belongs to you. Here's my story.

The anticipation had been building for a week. My best friend Linda said her sister Connie (sounds like a country-western song) would be a delightful, interesting house guest. Connie was the owner of a massage and wellness business. She was a sharp contrast to me with my fairly predictable financial services jobs. Linda described Connie as someone who can read the body's chakras — someone who can nearly read another person's mind.

So, there we sat — just the two of us — at my kitchen island visiting and learning more about how we spent our day. Connie's day was remarkably interesting. She hosted a booth at a wellness convention. Connie shared with me some palm reading she had done that morning for one lady in particular. Amazing. Tearful. Powerful. I was soaking up everything Connie had to share. Connie was insightful. She was a master in her craft. She was clearly an authority in wellness. And, the more we talked, I was certain that Connie would know the answer to my question.

So, I popped it to her, "Will I be a CEO one day Connie? Will I?"

In her calm, melodic voice Connie answered with a simple, "No."

Suddenly, I judged Connie as incompetent. Of course, I was going to be a CEO. That was my next career step and I could taste it. I'd been preparing for that job for years. The startled look on my face signaled Connie to deliver her second sentence. She said, "No, because you are destined for something much greater." My mind was exploding as I processed her explanation. It scared me. Somehow, I managed to bring the late-night conversation to a close and ran to bed to cover my head. Connie had unknowingly severely rocked my world. She delivered a 20.0 earthquake to my career path toward which I had been working and mapping out so carefully and thoughtfully.

Fast forward to six years. I had intentionally shifted my path away from being a CEO inspiring one organization, to developing my professional speaking capabilities to inspire thousands of people. There I was delivering the keynote speech to a large conference audience. I was on that stage to inspire the audience to act — to embrace change and move forward.

After that speech, I called Connie from the convention center parking lot in Las Vegas. I wanted her to be the first one to hear that I finally understood what she said to me that night in the kitchen. There was something much greater in this world for me, and I wanted to share just how I had discovered what that was.

I told Connie that on that stage, I felt my authentic self. I could feel the universe sending me a million signals that I'm on this earth to encourage and inspire others — millions of others. I could be my authentic self and share that self to inspire others to stand in their own authentic power, too. Thank you, Connie.

Looking back, I learned that my path to my authentic self wasn't the one I originally mapped out and created for myself. Instead, my path came to life, because Connie challenged me to think bigger.

YOUR AUTHENTIC SELF: MAY I CHALLENGE YOU

Are you on your comfortable path? Are you on a path that others created for you? Or, are you on your true path to your authentic self? Are you thinking big enough for yourself?

In this chapter, we will:

- Look at what fuels the authentic self and how you determine your gifts
- Understand what it means to own what you own
- Explore a client's story to illustrate how knowing your gifts and talents can put you in the driver's seat for your next promotion
- Add a sanity check to keep you in balance as you're finding your way
- In closing, how to speak and write in your unique voice to establish your authority

YOUR AUTHENTIC SELF: HOW TO FIND IT

It's time to stop feeling small.

The authentic self loves honesty. It digs transparency. And, it really thrives on accountability. These three things — honesty, transparency, and accountability — keep us grounded in our own personal, authentic power.

To nourish your authentic self, you openly talk to the voices in your head each night. And, own what you own. Let me explain.

What makes you unique? When I first met my book coach Cathy, I introduced myself as The Denise. And I quickly went on to say that

Cathy was The Cathy. Adding The underscores the uniqueness in all of us.

What makes you *The* (insert your name here)?

Too often things come so naturally to us that we do three things:

- We don't see nor recognize them
- We don't place enough value in/on them
- We bury them to fit in

Why? Because when you really own what you own, you begin to ignite your own authentic power. Your gifts are your own and they belong uniquely to you. You've been taught to be humble and not blow your own horn. So, owning your gifts can make you feel boastful. Let's work to turn that around — to change the way you own what you own.

Are you good with people? Details? Planning? Talking? Listening? What's important is that you self-identify with a shortlist of attributes that come easy to you. Take a blank piece of paper (physical or electronic) and write three bullet points that describe your gifts — these also can be things that others call on you to do. If your mind is blank, it's important that you stretch yourself and write something down. Perfect won't get you an A+ here. This is your private list.

What's on your shortlist? *Own what you own.*

YOUR AUTHENTIC SELF: PUT YOURSELF IN THE DRIVER'S SEAT FOR YOUR NEXT PROMOTION

Here's the practical application for identifying your gifts and *owning* what you own. Consider my client. Her boss asked her to come to a meeting to answer the career question, what do you want to do? In her case, the organization was dealing with rapid growth and was realigning departments and resources.

As we broke down the question, so she could prepare her answer, she realized that she needed to simply answer the question. What do you want to do? She wanted to use her gifts and talents. She wanted a job that enabled her to use her talent. She didn't just want a *job*.

She told her boss that she was an excellent problem solver and communicator with the ability to pull people together to collaborate and get things done. She was open to being strategically realigned wherever the boss needed this type of talent.

What happened? She got a promotion. She laid out what she needed and wanted and owned what she owns. The boss was delighted with a refreshing conversation with an employee who wasn't vying for a job, but rather a position. She clearly demonstrated she was a team player and was pliable. In the end, the two of them co-created a position that maximized her talent and she was promoted.

YOUR AUTHENTIC SELF: KEEPING YOUR BALANCE AS YOU'RE FINDING YOUR WAY

For some reason, we move through our childhood with great joy playing simple games. Imaginations run wild when we're wearing a size 4T. We're delighted to be playing with simple boxes and rubber bands. We find joy in some unusual places. Then, as we get older, we start to mold ourselves to fit in. We start to modify our authentic self to be more like what we see around us. To be more like who we think we should be.

Trying too hard to be something — anything — is exhausting.

You don't want to wake up like Maggie Carpenter. Maggie is the character in the movie *Runaway Bride* played by Julia Roberts. Maggie's fiancé, Ike Graham played by Richard Gere, challenges her that she doesn't even know how she likes her eggs prepared. He delivers the blow that she likes her eggs whatever style her boyfriend likes. Hard-boiled. Fried. Scrambled. Clearly, Maggie has lost her balance and her authentic self.

Spoiler — Maggie works to regain her authentic self and in fact, she likes her eggs "Benedict" a dish that features poached eggs over bacon and buttered English muffin with Hollandaise sauce. Maggie did the work and went deep on identifying her authentic self — who she is and what she enjoys. The Maggie regained her balance.

Trying to be the *most liked* isn't staying true to your authentic self either. Once you start building this absurd will-they-like-me radar, you start losing your footing. You start losing your balance. You start drifting away from your authentic self and you sabotage your authority. You start thinking in terms of if/then far too much. If I do this, then she will like me more.

You can get so good at overusing this will-they-like-me radar to the point where you don't even know you're using it. And, what's more, you don't even know that you've lost your way in delivering your authentic self.

How do you know when you're losing your balance? When do you know if you're not standing in your own power and delivering your authentic self? Here's your sanity check. Here's the single question to determine if you're trying too hard to be the most liked. Why did I do that?

If you answer by saying, "I wanted to." That's good. You genuinely, simply wanted to. End of report. End of drama.

However, if you pause in any way and say something like, "I thought (insert almost anything here)," then you're on your way to losing your authentic self.

Being authentic must feel right to you. You should never feel like you're exhausted and working too hard to be you. There is only one you — be YOU.

For me, I know I'm being *The Denise* — the person who is on this earth to encourage and inspire others — when I *feel* the opportunity to inspire every day. When I find ways to inspire myself. When I find something positive in *everything*. When I can poke fun at my own shortcomings. When I speak my mind and state my opinions. When I'm around other people always looking for what makes them unique. When I'm the best leader I can be. Every. Single. Day.

YOUR AUTHENTIC SELF: HOW TO SPEAK AND WRITE IN YOUR VOICE

You are unique. You have a unique voice. It belongs to you and only you. Use it. Every time you speak or write, use your voice. Establish your brand. Voice your opinions. Pen your thoughts. Establish your authority.

As I was writing my first book, I somehow started using too much corporate speak. My book coach said, "There's only one you and I want to read the book by *The Denise*, not by some boring executive." Yes, I snapped out of it. I started recording and transferring speech to text. I started each of my writing blocks by writing case studies as those were easier for me to write in my voice. Once I established my voice, I would keep pounding the keys. I would sit on our patio swing — with the leopard cushions — and read out loud what I had written. Then, I could hear where I needed to edit. I was always open to inviting improvements from others — making the edits in my voice.

Remember, everything you do carries your signature — your authentic self. Your authentic self is where your authority lives. Standing in your authentic power should be effortless. Own what you own.

Want more? See http://thedenise.com/ to be encouraged and inspired.

CHAPTER 10

FOPO: Fear of People's Opinions

Jason B. A. Van Camp

Business Growth Strategist

 https://www.linkedin.com/in/jason-van-camp-076a5339/

 www.missionsixzero.com

 www.warriorrising.org

Jason B.A. Van Camp is a decorated Green Beret, world traveler, entrepreneur, author, and loyal friend. Born in Washington, D.C., and raised across the Potomac River in Springfield, Virginia, Jason attended and played football at the United States Military Academy at West Point.

After graduation, Jason earned his U.S. Army Ranger tab and Special Forces tab and began serving as a Detachment Commander with 10th Special Forces Group in Fort Carson, Colorado.

Jason deployed to war zones in the Middle East and Africa, receiving three Bronze Stars, one with a "V device" for Valor. Jason currently resides near Salt Lake City, Utah, and is married to his wife, Elizabeth. Together, they have a little girl, Claire Jane, and a boy, Jackson Jason.

"**L**et me get this straight, Jason. You are starting a leadership consulting business?" asked my favorite BYU Master of Business Administration (MBA) professor. His condescension and disappointment invited an unhealthy level of discomfort in sharp opposition to my bullish optimism.

While considering my rebuttal, I slowly brushed some dust off the seat of a leather chair across from his desk and sat down.

"I get the sense that you don't think too highly of my business idea, sir," I said.

He didn't pick up on my sarcasm.

My professor rubbed the back of his neck and took off his reading glasses. Pushing his chair away from his desk slightly, he slowly and deliberately chose his next words, "Jason, we could find you a high-paying job working just about anywhere. Why do you want to start a leadership business? I mean, leadership of all things?"

"My mother always used to say, 'Show me your friends and I'll show you your future.' Well, all my friends are successful entrepreneurs. They have shown me that it's possible. If those idiots can do it, so can I."

He didn't laugh.

"No, what I mean is, what makes you the authority on leadership?" he replied.

"Well, I'm pretty knowledgeable and passionate about leadership, sir," I countered.

"How so?" he interjected, probing further.

"Well, I attended West Point — the premiere leadership academy in the world. I was an officer in the U.S. Army Special Forces, leading my team on 300 combat operations during three deployments to the Middle East."

He shrugged his shoulders and simply said, "Eh, I just don't see how that makes you interesting or knowledgeable about leadership."

I swallowed my anger but realized he had a point. Kind of.

He continued without waiting for a response, "Jason, I just... I just don't know of any business like this ever succeeding without first having some kind of material."

"What do you mean, sir?" I asked.

"What I'm getting at is you need to write a book first. That's how it's done in this business. Jason, I highly recommend you write a book," my professor urged me. "Writing your own book will build your reputation, give you credibility, and make you the subject matter expert. Essentially, you will be the authority in whatever leadership category you wish to pursue because you literally wrote the book on it."

"Can I possibly emphasize *"highly recommend"* enough?" he admonished.

I leaned back in the leather chair. "Sir, I'm just not ready to write a book. I don't have business experience, yet. Plus, I'm a Green Beret and we are known as 'Quiet Professionals.' I can't put myself out there. I don't want people to get the wrong impression. I don't want to bring attention to myself."

"Jason, you shouldn't look at it that way. If you have something to say, don't be afraid to say it. Your group's nickname is 'Quiet Professionals' not 'silent professionals.' Starting a business with no material or marketing is seldom a recipe for success. You can't be an authority if no one knows about you."

"I understand, sir. With all due respect, I will take your advice into consideration."

My professor put his glasses back on and stared at me in silence for a full five seconds. Blowing out a disapproving sigh, he simply responded, "Okay, I wish you the best of luck." We shook hands and I walked out of his office, leaving his door open. I glanced back at him and noticed that he was back to typing on his computer, shaking his head.

Deep down, I knew he was speaking the truth. But, "MAN! Aghhhh!" I don't want to put myself out there. I don't want to do it."

Do you ever feel yourself saying those exact words to yourself?

I know I must do it, but I really don't want to.

We've all been there.

We don't want to accept it. We wrestle with the truth in our mind. We tend to experience cognitive dissonance since thoughts are usually easier to change than behavior. We alter our mindset saying things like, "If I start marketing myself, I am going to come across as arrogant, pretentious, and self-promoting... which also is bad."

Once we accept that we are likely wrong about our assumptions and that, in fact, we can market ourselves, our companies, and our brands in an authentic and effective way, we tend to procrastinate. When we procrastinate, we don't push back on the execution of the task itself, we delay or push back feeling the emotion associated with the execution of the task.

Personally, social media is an example where I've encountered strong personal reluctance. Posting on social media is as simple as selecting a picture or video, uploading it to the social media platform, typing a caption, and posting. The process is simple, but it creates a feeling of anxiety. We push back on that anxiety. We don't fear the task itself, we fear the emotion associated with the task.

Once we are able to overcome that anxiety, that fear, we make a decision. Eventually, we choose to accept and take action.

Looking back on this experience, I honestly ask myself, "Why did I not want to... write a book? Market myself? Post on Social Media?"

What was I afraid of?

Enter: *FOPO*

Definition: *Fear of People's Opinions*

As much as FOMO (fear of missing out) is social anxiety stemming from the belief that others might be having more fun than you, I was experiencing **FOPO**. An anxiety that you have when you want to say something (or post something online), but the possible negative consequences are so overwhelming that you don't say (or post) anything.

I was afraid of what other people would think about me. I was afraid of what they would say about me. I was afraid of them creating a new identity for me, better still, changing the way I think about myself.

I didn't feel free. I felt shackled. I realized that if you care about what other people think about you, you always will be their prisoner. I was a coward. And, being a coward definitely is not who I am.

A few years into my business, I was consulting with a young female executive in New York. With tears and frustration in her eyes, she said, "I feel like an imposter at my new position. I'm a brand-new leader and I'm on the verge of being exposed. Can you help me stop feeling like such a fraud?!"

"Well, first of all, everything is going to be alright. What you are feeling is **FOPO — Fear of Other People's Opinions** and it's very common. In your situation, what we are talking about is leadership," I explained. "It's about influencing and inspiring people to be the best they can be. When you're a new leader, you aren't expected to know everything. You are expected to be humble and willing to learn."

I continued, "I'll tell you what you need to do to succeed, but it's going to be uncomfortable."

Holding back tears, she said, "I'm willing to do whatever it takes."

"The first thing I want you to do is tell your people who you are, what your values are, and what you believe in. Next, I want you to flat out tell them that you aren't going to pretend that you are someone that you aren't. Tell them you don't have all the answers. (Spoiler alert — they already know that.) Tell them that you are there to learn from them. Tell them that you are going to ask questions. Tell them that you are going to listen to their opinions and make the best decision for the company based on your judgment."

Tell them that you are there for <u>them</u>.

Tell them your priorities (in this order):

1. Mission
2. Team
3. Teammates
4. Self

"Understanding what is important and prioritizing those things is one of the most important lessons I learned as a Green Beret in the U.S. Army Special Forces. When you expose your heart and tell them these things, you are going to be nervous, you are going to be scared, and you are going to be uncomfortable. You will think that by telling them these things, it is going to hurt you. It's actually going to help you. You are going to begin to embrace a mindset of becoming 'selfish about being selfless.'"

The young executive continued cautiously, "Jason, I want to trust you, but how do I know what you are saying is true? How will I know that it is working?"

"You know it's working when you see results," I stated.

Continuing on, I told her, "When I began my career as a leadership development consultant, I had to speak... a lot. When I first started out, it was rough. I wasn't very good. But, I kept grinding. I learned and improved. Seemingly, all of a sudden, people started coming up to me after keynote presentations and thanking me. It was then that I started to see results. It was then that I realized the process was working."

"When I was approached following keynote presentations, all I had to do was look into their eyes to know their words of gratitude were coming from a place of sincerity. It was real. I was told that what I said impacted them in a profoundly positive way.

Similar to being a leader in the military, I felt like I was once again serving others. That feeling of service became infectious. I wanted to continue serving. In parallel, on social media, random people started sending me private messages expressing authentic appreciation for my posts. I was seeing results and that gave me the confidence to keep going. I was defeating my fear."

After a few months of coaching this young executive through this process and empowering her to overcome **FOPO**, she sent me this message: "Jason, I am bubbling over with enthusiasm. Your advice worked! Thank you so much! It's not only that I want to be a better leader, but you actually changed my life! What I didn't realize was how real the connections became between me and my team. Don't be afraid of sharing your story. It will help others!"

Taking the advice of my BYU MBA professor from eight years before, I finally created my "material." I wrote a book about my experiences in the military and in business entitled, *Deliberate Discomfort: How US Special Operations Forces Overcome Fear and Dare to Win by Getting Comfortable Being Uncomfortable.* I've found that this book is by far the most powerful way to communicate my message. I became the authority on getting comfortable being uncomfortable.

Why am I the authority? Because I wasn't afraid to be.

I overcame my fear and wrote a book. My book became a bestseller. I overcame my fear and started to market myself and my company on social media. It's still uncomfortable for me, but it's only through deliberate discomfort that we can grow, learn, and become stronger.

I overcame my **FOPO** and was rewarded for it.

After all, somebody's got to be the authority, why not me?

CHAPTER 11

The Value of
Writing a Book

Mark Leonard

Book Coach

 linkedin.com/in/markcleonard

 https://CartwrightPublishing.com

Mark put himself through Davidson College in North Carolina by starting and running a landscaping business. After obtaining his MBA from the Darden School at the University of Virginia, he moved out West. He first lived in South Lake Tahoe, where he invested in real estate and started a real estate videotaping company.

That got wiped out in the early '80s as interest rates spiked to 18%, so he moved to the San Francisco Bay Area. There he landed a job at ROLM Corporation, holding positions in corporate finance, project management, and sales.

He then held senior positions in a number of software companies involved in the chip design market, followed by a stint as a retained recruiter in the professional services arena.

Following that, he and his wife invested in Subway™ franchises. They sold those stores after five years and wrote a book about that experience, revealing information that is typically very difficult to obtain. That led to requests to help others write and publish their books, and he has been helping non-fiction authors ever since.

Mark can be reached at (415) 250-6343, or by visiting Cartwright Publishing.com.

In 2002, Joseph Epstein of *The New York Times* published a study revealing that "81 percent of Americans feel that they have a book in them — and should write it." Today, that's approaching 200 million Americans over the age of 18! But, why would people write books, especially in this age of instant, on-demand content?

There already are more than 4.5 million books on Amazon, probably written by two to three million authors. Some published studies indicate that the average lifetime sales per book are 250, and that is probably skewed high because of the handful of authors who sell more than 100,000 books. So, the likelihood of any author making money from selling books is very small. Given these rather depressing statistics, why would anyone spend the time and effort to write a book?

I am a book coach and publisher who helps authors write their books, get them published, and have them become bestsellers. With only a little bit of tongue-in-cheek, I promise my clients that the income from their book sales will NOT even begin to cover the cost of my services! Sounds like a strange sales pitch, doesn't it? But, it is the truth. So, why would anyone agree to this rather strange arrangement where the author not only is working really hard (writing a book is hard. Period) but paying a bunch of money on top of it? The answers vary, and it turns out that it's not quite as crazy as it seems. I thought the best way to illustrate this would be to highlight a number of my clients' stories and how writing and publishing a book, or multiple books, brought significant value to them in a variety of ways.

Author Paul Svec and I worked together in the telecommunications sphere back in the 1980s. Several years later, he started a company in the San Francisco Bay Area that catered to the telecom needs of small and medium-sized businesses (SMBs). All SMBs need an array of the services that Paul's company provided, such as telephone systems, WiFi, data networking, cabling, and more, which is a field that constantly is evolving. The challenge that Paul faced, given that he was an SMB himself, is that his customers rarely had the expertise to evaluate all the choices they had, and so the sales process typically was long and complicated.

I suggested he write a book that explained telecommunications technology in enough detail to provide a decision-maker with enough information that they could make reasonable decisions. He agreed, and we got busy writing the book. After we finished this fairly dry and technical book, *Make Your Small Business Communications Ecosystem Thrive*, we looked at each other, laughed, and said "We'll probably be the only two people on the planet who will read this book."

However, Paul started handing it out to prospective customers who were impressed that Paul was a published author and not just a sales guy, which helped him establish his authority. Then he related a remarkable story to me. He had given his book to a prospective customer who didn't have much knowledge of the telecom field and when he had a face-to-face meeting with her two weeks later, he observed that his book was highlighted, had notes all over it, and the prospect had a number of incisive questions that enabled them to immediately propose a configuration.

The prospect signed a contract the next week, shaving months of the typical sales cycle, and obtained the sale with minimum effort. *The value?* Shortening the sales cycle, and reducing the sales effort.

My next story is about inventor Roger Sramek. Roger had a number of patents to his name and was excited about his latest invention, which could improve the lives of many people around the world. He had invented and patented a unique mattress that kept the sleeper's spine in alignment all night long, no matter the sleeper's position.

This resulted in a deeper, more restful sleep, which is clinically proven to provide significant health benefits, including a more robust immune system, weight loss, increased energy, and freedom from pain. I helped Roger write an engaging book, *Your Sleep: Wake Up Refreshed!* about the power and benefits, this mattress could provide.

As a result of becoming a published author, he was able to secure a number of speaking engagements with audiences interested in this topic. After one of his talks, a member of the audience came up to meet him and identified himself as a potential investor. Weeks later, they negotiated a significant deal potentially worth millions of dollars. *The value?* Becoming an authoritative speaker, and securing venture capital.

My next author, Registered Investment Advisor (RIA) Scott G. Eichler, was a financial advisor in Southern California. Like most financial advisors, Scott was seeking to grow his practice and clientele in an extremely competitive environment. He observed that while most financial advisors had slick marketing brochures, himself included, almost no one had written a book about financial investing.

Scott had a way of explaining investing that was both clear and refreshing, so we got busy and wrote his book, *Don't Play Chicken with Your Nest Egg.* When he began to use his book as his calling card, he found that prospective investors resonated with the content and that being a published author was a competitive advantage. *The value?* Gain authority in a competitive market.

Christopher Hanson, Esq., is a prominent California commercial real estate litigation attorney. He's the guy to call when things get really ugly because he is one of a few lawyers who relishes going to court and fighting for his clients in front of a judge and jury — and he's very good at it.

The challenge Mr. Hanson experienced was staying top-of-mind with all the real estate brokerage firms, so that when a deal went south, he would be the attorney they thought to call. After discussing his marketing strategy, we decided to create a book by videotaping Mr. Hanson discussing the most important cases in California real estate litigation, and then transcribing those videos into a book, *War Story Wednesdays.*

This had the advantage of populating his website and YouTube channels with engaging content where the viewer could get a real sense of Mr. Hanson's style. In addition, he used the book in his outreach efforts by sending copies every week to brokerage offices throughout the state, as well as seeking speaking engagements on the topic of what to do if litigation became imminent. *The value?* Combining a book with video and social media to increase visibility as an authority in your market.

Ken Matejka, J.D., LL.M., is an attorney who specializes in an entirely different practice. Ken, who obviously is a lawyer himself, helps law firms use Google marketing to generate leads. This is critically important, especially for small- and medium-sized firms competing against giants. Before writing his book, Ken used his internet marketing skills to gain leads.

Then I worked with Ken on publishing his book, *The Lawyer's Ultimate Guide to Online Leads,* and he started sending free copies of the book to prospective clients. This proved to be so successful that, ironically for an online marketing advisor, this is now the only marketing that Ken does! *The value?* Obtain new clients by sending prospects a free copy of your book.

Matthew Le Merle and his wife, Alison Davis, are two of the world's most preeminent technology angel investors and corporate consultants. Matthew heard me speak about the power of being an author and asked me to join him for coffee.

It turns out that he was a prolific writer and had published many articles over the years, but his challenge and frustration was that he hadn't been able to sit down and write a book. As I listened to Matthew discuss his ideas, I suggested that he wasn't talking about one book — he was talking about multiple books! His audiences were different and his messages were different, so he needed to break them into separate books.

He realized right there what had been stopping him, and we then got to work. Within 90 days, we published his and Alison's first book, *Build Your Fortune in the Fifth Era*, aimed at accredited investors who had not yet taken advantage of investing in tech startups. Then 30 days later, we followed up with their second book, *Corporate Innovation in the Fifth Era*, aimed at executives in the Fortune 500 who were looking for strategic guidance on how to keep up with and implement rapid technological change.

We followed up the publication of the written books with releasing the audio versions of the books, which used professional voice artists. *The value?* Both books raised their visibility and authoritative presence in their respective markets, and they were able to significantly expand their speaking opportunities, consulting engagements, and investor interest.

The next author I'd like to highlight had a completely different motivation for wanting to write and publish his books. He is a highly successful breast-cancer surgeon in the Phoenix area and has saved many lives throughout his long and illustrious career. He didn't want to write a book to gain more patients nor to enhance his career opportunities.

Instead, he wanted to leave a legacy for his family, especially his grandchildren, and to inspire immigrants who had a dream of becoming successful in the United States. You see, Dr. Edgar Hernandez was born in a dirt-floor home on the Pacific coast of Southern Mexico, and at the age of eight, he had a dream of becoming not only a surgeon but a surgeon in the United States.

After his beloved father passed away when Edgar was just nine years old, he left his mother and his cherished family behind and immigrated to the U.S. at the age of 10. Through hard work and determination, and perhaps divine intervention, he not only achieved his goal of becoming a surgeon, but he also was able to bring his mother and much of his family to join him in becoming U.S. citizens.

He now has written three books and is working on his fourth. His first book, *On the Border of a Dream*, is his story of coming to the U.S. and achieving his dream of becoming a surgeon. His second book, *Earth Angel with a Green Card*, is about the role his angelic mother played not only in his life but in the lives of so many others'. His third book, *Miguel Hernandez - Mystic*, is about his stepbrother who made his own, as well as many others' journeys possible.

His fourth book will be about his father, who was a remarkable healer and inspired Edgar to become a doctor. *The value?* Dr. Hernandez's remarkable life story is now an inspiration for his family and anyone else who wants to achieve the American dream.

These stories illustrate the diverse ways in which becoming a published author can increase the author's authority. Yes, it can help the author's business in many ways, including shortening the sales cycle, improving sales productivity, raising capital, gaining new clients, leveraging social media, increasing visibility, and obtaining speaking engagements, among others. Perhaps leaving a legacy that will last for decades is the crowning achievement of becoming a published author.

Chapter 12

How to Leverage an 800-Pound Gorilla to Become an Authority

Melanie Johnson

Publishing, Marketing and Brand Expert

 https://www.linkedin.com/in/melaniejohnson-eop/

https://www.instagram.com/eliteonlinepublishing/

https://www.youtube.com/watch?v=aXyLNrnl7OE

https://eliteonlinepublishing.com/

Melanie Churella Johnson is a 14-time best-selling author. She is a speaker, coach, and consultant. Melanie was honored to be a TEDx speaker where she spoke on the importance of leaving a legacy: "Leaving a Legacy - The Time is Now". She has owned and operated two independent TV stations in Houston and Dallas. She has been in front of and behind the camera.

Melanie started her career as a News Anchor in Detroit at Channel 20 after she won the title of Miss Michigan and was the first runner up to Miss America. She is currently the owner of Elite Online Publishing and Charity Auction Consignments. She is passionate about sharing people's stories that, educate, motivate, and inspire. She is an expert at publishing, marketing, and positioning nonfiction books for business owners and professionals. She creates expert authority status for marketing impact and influence. She is honored to work one on one with her authors to create the best strategies for book creation, marketing, and social media.

She is the host of the podcast "Elite Expert Insider" on iTunes and Stitcher Radio. Melanie is the single mom with two teenage boys and resided in Houston Texas.

W ouldn't it be nice if you could hire Amazon to promote you and your business for free?

Wouldn't it be nice if Amazon recommended your work to the millions on their email list for free?

Wouldn't it be nice if Amazon gave you a page on their website to post videos, photos, a bio, an RSS feed of your blog or podcast? Also, what if Amazon included all your social media links and website links to buy your products or services, shown on the first page of Google search... all for free?

YOU CAN HAVE ALL OF THIS. ALL YOU HAVE TO DO IS WRITE AND PUBLISH A BOOK ON AMAZON.

If you haven't noticed, according to Forbes, Amazon is the #1 retailer in the world and Jeff Bezos is the richest man in the world.

Out of almost seven billion people in the world, only about 500,000 will publish a book each year and take advantage of the power of Amazon. When you publish a book you become part of an ELITE group.

Hands down, in my opinion, there is no better way to establish your brand, tell your story, create business awareness, become an authority, and gain die-hard fans, than publishing a book.

Ask yourself... does your competition have a book? If not, you're ahead of the game.

Here are some serious questions for you, if you really want to be known as an authority.

- Are you considered in the top 5% of your niche?
- Do you want to attract high-quality clients?
- Do you want to make a powerful, long-lasting difference?

By becoming a bestselling author you can leverage your knowledge effectively to reach more people, make more money, and make a powerful difference in the world. By leveraging Amazon you are using one of the most powerful search engines and retailers in the world.

Amazon has 50% or more of the U.S. print book market , and at least three-quarters of publishers' eBook sales (it also has its own eBook publishing business, for which it has never disclosed any data). In comparison, Walmart has 9%. Data from Civic Science shows 47% of all consumer product searches start on Amazon.

When you become an author, Amazon gives you an Amazon Author page for FREE and promotes it for FREE.

LET'S TALK ABOUT AN AMAZON AUTHOR PAGE AND WHY YOU NEED ONE.

An Amazon Author Page is one of the most powerful tools in Google search. This Author page (if filled in appropriately) always will show up on the first page and usually one of the top three on the first page of a Google search for your name, book, or company.

It's like having Amazon working for you for FREE. It is the most powerful search engine on the planet.

An Amazon Author page is one of the easiest ways to allow others to discover you and your company. It is also the perfect place for you to connect with your readers, clients, and media, so they can get to know you personally. This establishes your online presence in a way most other routes can't.

New York Times Bestselling Author, Loral Langemeier, was published by a traditional publishing house and her Amazon Author Page was basically empty. It didn't have all of her books linked to it. None of her publishers did this for her. It's like having a Facebook page that's almost blank. She hired our company, Elite Online Publishing, to correct it for her. Now her Amazon Author Page rocks, with links to all her products, services, websites, and social media.

WHAT YOU CAN ADD ON YOUR AMAZON AUTHOR PAGE:

- Link your blog posts, Podcast, or any RSS feed
- Post up to eight videos
- Post up to eight photos
- Link your social media accounts
- Link your website
- Link your products or services
- Develop a strategic biography
- Current and past events

Not only can readers, clients, and media get to know you and your books through this page, it can connect them with your other content, such as blog posts, Twitter, Instagram feed, photos, videos, links to other social media, and more.

Your story matters, so you deserve an audience. Connecting with a broad audience can be difficult on your own, with an Amazon Author Page, you increase your discoverability. Because of the search algorithm, your book is more likely to be seen if you have an Amazon Author Page. The more active you are on your account, the greater the likelihood that your book will appear. Amazon always will link your name to your Amazon Author Page, if someone is looking at just one book, they are connected to all of the material and content you have available to them. There is also a Follow feature linked to your Amazon Author Page, readers can receive notifications every time you publish something new.

When you have a TV or Podcast interview, they ask for your photo, bio, social media, links, your book description, and any videos of you speaking at events. Guess what? All of this is on your Amazon Author Profile. You can copy and send the link and voilà, it's all done.

Check out my Amazon Author Page and that of my business partner, Jenn Foster, to give you two good examples of what an effective author page looks like:

Amazon.com/author/jennfoster and Amazon.com/authormelaniejohnson.

BENEFITS OF AN AMAZON AUTHOR PAGE:

- It is a free platform
- You show up on the first page of Google search
- Fan base can follow you; fans are notified each time you publish a new book
- Keeps content fresh and new with the RSS feed of your blog or podcast
- You have complete control of this page
- Improves Amazon searches
- Connects you with more readers
- Builds your following of readers
- Post eight videos: videos that brand you, give you credibility, or help sell products or services
- Post eight photos
- Perfect place to host your bio (update quarterly or as events change in your life)

With all these amazing benefits, why wouldn't you want to write and publish a book, as well as create an Amazon Author Page? It's the perfect resource for any individual or company.

Another great way for Amazon to take notice of you is to make your book a #1 Bestseller.

When you publish your book, make sure your publisher guarantees they will make you a bestselling author. We have made every single book we have published #1 in multiple categories.

WHY BECOME A #1 BESTSELLER?

The reason it's important to become a "#1 Bestselling Author" is that it substantially increases your credibility and "personal brand". It can establish you as a thought leader and business influencer. You are able to show that you not only wrote a book but that the market has voted it better than the other books out there. It's a status symbol, people of all ages are impressed with still today. I've personally become a #1 Bestseller 14 times. It's a coveted title that not just anyone can achieve.

Becoming a bestseller gives you extra credibility, which says to a new client or media outlet that your book is not only a bestseller, but people like it. Once you have #1 Bestselling status, it's a title you keep forever. Your great-grandchildren will brag that you were a bestselling author. It's a legacy of authority that lasts a lifetime.

A pastor of my church in Houston, with a congregation of more than 40,000 people, published a book with a faith-based publishing house. He launched his book hoping for great success and promoted it in the bulletin, the church newsletter, at three services for two Sundays in a row. I had just started in the publishing business. My two sons and I attended the evening service the following Sunday, which is a little more laid back, and he announced then that he was #1... to his family and friends. Sadly, his book did not hit #1 on Amazon charts. My sons were elbowing me, "Mom you need to help him and make him a #1 Bestseller." Sadly, I could never get past his gatekeeper to help him and his book. The moral of the story is to make sure you work with a great publisher that **will guarantee** they will make you a #1 Bestselling Author. You've invested all the time and energy to write the book, it's worth going the extra mile to make sure it hits #1.

12 COSTLY MISTAKES WHEN CHOOSING A PUBLISHER.

THE OTHER 800-POUND GORILLA

GOOGLE

Ninety-four percent of all searches happen on a Google property, according to Jumpshot. What does Google love the most? Fresh content.

One of the best ways to create fresh content is by repurposing the content from your book.

Authority also comes from writing articles, blog posts, social media posts, and podcasts. By becoming a Bestselling Author you will have enough fresh content to create about 200 articles, 2,000 blog posts, and 200-300 podcasts, plus enough material to talk about while being interviewed on other people's podcasts.

When you are publishing a book, use it to grow your business and expand your influence. The authority that comes with a book will help you generate new leads, close more deals, develop income for your business, and will be a powerful marketing asset.

When a customer comes to you after reading your book, they generally are more valuable than customers that come from other means. They usually take less time in the sales cycle and have a higher customer value over time.

One of our authors, Josh Evans, decided he wanted to leave his day job as a sales rep. The first thing he did was to write a book that would identify him as an expert in his field of consulting and speaking. Elite Online Publishing made his book a #1 Bestseller the day of the launch. This immediately propelled his career as a speaker and corporate motivator, commanding five-figures for his services. He even spoke on the Queen Mary.

Once you become a #1 Bestselling Author, Google takes notice and you could get a **Google Knowledge Panel**. What is a Google Knowledge Panel, you may ask?

"Have you ever Googled an artist or business/brand and saw the right-side panel that offers various links, a bio, photos, and more? That's called a Google Knowledge Panel and it is an absolute necessity if you represent a professional online brand" — source: *https://millennialmoderator.com*.

Google Knowledge Panels provide a "business card" for you or your brand, they also improve your SEO (Search Engine Optimization).

To get a Google Knowledge Panel, you must show Google that you have (valid) content about yourself on the internet. Once you are a #1 Bestselling Author and you've repurposed that content on social media, articles, etc., Google's Knowledge Panel will take notice.

The following are five reasons to become an author and get a Google Knowledge Panel:

- Increased organic search on Google
- Google brand reputation and authority
- Higher ranking in Google search results
- Self-posting on Google
- Cross-promotion on Google

According to Aleksey Weyman from Millennial Moderator
https://millennialmoderator.com

If you ever had any doubt about the power of becoming an author to make you an authority in your field, I'm sure you are now realizing the benefits of leveraging the 800-pound gorillas — Amazon and Google — that will take you, your brand, and your business to the next level, all at no additional cost to you. Take advantage of the opportunity.

I think it's so important that you leverage the power of authorship to gain authority, after all, the word *author* is part of *author*ity.

Here is a free gift to get you started.

Get our FREE BOOK *Accomplishment and Personal Success Story Starter* by texting your name and email to: 832-572-5285

CHAPTER 13

The New Age of Authority

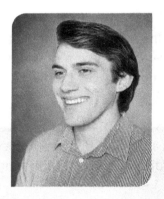

Social Media Advertising and Brand Specialist

https://www.instagram.com/weekdayrehab/

Nathan Johnson has recently been named one of Yahoo's "Top 15 Young Entrepreneurs of 2020," along with being interviewed by the New York Times earlier this year.

Coming in at number 7 on Yahoo's list, the Baylor University junior Finance and Management double major has been growing his business since he was twelve.

He now boasts an Instagram account portfolio of over 10 million total followers, along with previous consulting work with prominent names in social media, such as David Dobrik and Yung Gravy.

He has founded ONLY MEDIA LLC., an advertising agency that encompasses all of his ventures, and continues to work on increasing his following and establishing new brands.

There are endless opinions in the world on what makes someone credible. Credibility is a word loosely thrown around everywhere, from television ads to everyday conversation. However, what exactly makes someone credible? As social media begins to take over the younger generation, credibility has started to morph into being more about one's online presence rather than offline merit. With so many major companies that are out of touch with the upcoming generation, now is the time to take advantage and evolve with the times. Remember Blockbuster?

At one point Blockbuster was THE largest retail store for purchasing and renting movies. However, when approached by Netflix and informed of the changing times of online purchases, they declined to make a change. Blockbuster has now been out of business for years and Netflix has created the model for streaming services around the world.

As an expert in social media, the biggest question I'm asked is: "How and why am I supposed to build my social media presence, I am a doctor/lawyer/real estate agent/etc.?" I will elaborate more later in this chapter, but my answer is always the same two-part response: have a game-plan and increase your credibility. As you read, though, keep an open mind. Envision your brand, company, or organization appearing on social media. What does that look like? What does that accomplish for you?

First, let's start with the How . For example, a streaming company approached me a year or so ago asking how they should start building their online presence. In all honesty, they were probably one of the more disconnected clients I have met so far, meaning they had not touched social media whatsoever for their company and did not know where to start. With this company, as well as all with whom I work, the beginning of their successful social media push always is having a game plan.

To which platforms do you want to market?

Answer that question for your own brand or company. This usually is dependent on your demographic. For example, if you market to those 18 and under, target Tik Tok; if it's 18 to 34-year-olds, target Instagram and Twitter; and for ages 34 and up, it's Facebook. Now, think of what you want the push to accomplish.

For my streaming service client, they wanted all demographics with an emphasis on those over 18, so the customer could purchase the subscription directly without having to consult a parent. Their entire marketing goal was to generate subscriptions and build their brand, along with establishing credibility. Once we agreed upon the game plan, it was time to execute.

Much like science, advertising on social media is a repetitive trial and error process until you find things that work. For the client in question, we tried comedy sketches, celebrity endorsements, and even free subscription giveaways. We saw conversions of course, but not what they wanted.

However, we finally found something that worked: Top 10's. With every client, I stress the value of creating an Instagram page for the brand. When people are comparing your product or service versus another, especially when they are aged 18 to 24, they almost always will look at your social media presence.

If you have a bigger presence than another brand, they will pick you every time. For this client, we came up with the idea to start creating Top 10 videos. For example, Top 10 Best Movie Moments, Top 10 Funniest Videos of the Month, and so forth. These videos started getting shared, saved, and seen by millions of people on Instagram and Tik Tok.

Instantly, their brand was established and self-sustaining on social media. Now, they have full-time employees running their Tik Tok and Instagram accounts, and credit a majority of their business to their social media presence.

Second, let's talk about the *Why*. Even though it seems apparent already as to *why* you should build up your social media presence, I always find it helpful to dive into specifics. One of the best reasons I can present is that, although I get paid by companies to build their social media following, you CAN do it completely *free.*

This day and age are all about viral content. If you want to get out there into the world, find someone, such as myself, who knows what content currently is going viral and brainstorm how you can do the same to be seen by millions for *free.*

For example, after you build your presence of about 10,000 followers, you now have 10,000 people who like you, your brand, product, service, etc. Whenever you post on social media from that point on, you have an influence on those 10,000 people. Every day, you can get the most targeted form of marketing possible for FREE just by posting creative videos or pictures.

Individuals and companies spend millions of dollars trying to get data on 10,000 people. Data such as who is interested in your product, what other things interest them, what are their hobbies, and so on, is invaluable as a part of advertising campaigns. If you achieve a 10,000-person following, you now have endless amounts of data regarding potential customers you can use to further expand your brand. Through the use of social media to gain credibility, you now have all that data for little-to-no money and very little time invested.

Another reason to place emphasis on a strong social media presence in building credibility is reaching the younger generation and how their brains are wired. As a member of Generation Z, I know that a majority of companies have no clue how young minds operate. The younger generation doesn't pay attention to billboards,

TV/radio commercials, nor really even any advertisements UNLESS they are tailored to the Gen Z liking or implemented into a form of content they enjoy (much like the Top 10 video series streaming service discussed earlier).

If you think a big advertising budget is going to save the day and get your social media credibility up, enjoy as you watch your ad seen by millions, but interacted by none. Nothing can kill or revive a company faster than advertising, it has to be done right. A lot of companies and brands never properly include the younger generation, especially since a majority of Generation Z does not have the money nor ability to make their own decisions. However, now is the most important time to get in touch with Generation Z before you start losing money.

Your competitor is all over social media, and if you're still paying for TV ads in a few years, you are going to wish you had listened to my advice. As weird as it may sound, credibility is morphing into a sort of mob mentality concept. Here is what I mean by that: If a brand has millions of followers, in the mind of Generation Z, that means they are doing something right and are a good place to spend their money.

If we are talking about lawyers, members of Gen Z are more likely to trust a lawyer with millions of followers on Instagram, a verified blue checkmark, and a well thought out page, over someone who has 100 followers, no blue check, and a bio that says *Trustworthy Lawyer.*

As credibility and authority transform to comply with the new standards set by Generation Z, do NOT get left behind as the brand who can't accept the changing times. Social media is free to start and cheap to build up. If done properly, you can maximize profit, minimize expenses, and turn your company/brand into a well-respected business magnet.

Before I leave you to brainstorm what you can do on social media, I want to recommend a few inspirational examples of companies executing social media very well. The first, a fashion brand called Fashion Nova. They have more than 18 million followers on Instagram and have been paying Instagram pages and influencers since 2010 to wear their clothing and post pictures of themselves wearing the brand. Their unique advertising strategy turned them into a $150-million-dollar company.

Second, a doctor by the name of Dr. Miami. Dr. Miami decided to start posting surgery updates, office videos, and more on his Snapchat feed in early 2014. Ever since, he has created such a big following of potential clients that now his schedule is fully booked more than a year in advance.

Next, the dating app Hinge. Hinge has created multiple miniseries on their social media pages that go viral without Hinge spending any money, ranging from funniest first-date experiences to what to say and not to say on a date.

Finally, my personal favorite and the best company to look out for, Wendy's. Yes, the fast-food restaurant. Their social media presence has generated hundreds of million dollars in value. How? Well, they hired someone to run their social media. Their job was to make people laugh. They did this by essentially starting twitter arguments, cracking jokes, and even getting into funny exchanges with their followers. Here are a few examples of their tweets to give you a good laugh before I end my chapter:

Kai Lawns on twitter says: "@Wendys can you give me relationship advice?"

Wendy's Official Twitter says: "If you're asking a fast food twitter, then this relationship might be doomed"

Devon Peacock on Twitter says: "@Wendys how much does a big mac cost?"

Wendy's Official Twitter says: "Your dignity"

Phono on Twitter says: "@Wendys your food is trash"

Wendy's Official Twitter says: "No, your opinion is though"

All of these harmless, yet hysterical tweets, generated millions of eyeballs, tens of thousands of likes, retweets, and followers, along with establishing Wendy's as a social media giant and a legend amongst Generation Z.

My advice to all of you is to really think about how you could integrate social media into your advertising efforts. Even if this means working a little bit harder, it is going to be worth it in the long run.

Every single one of my clients comes back to tell me how grateful they are to have gotten into social media early. With virtually every brand making the shift to appeal to Generation Z, think about what it is that you need to do to achieve that same result and do it.

There is no better time than now. Every second you wait is a follower, dollar, or connection *lost*.

CHAPTER 14

The Force Multiplier: Why Authorship is the Ultimate Builder of Authority

Everett O'Keefe

International #1 Bestselling Author,
Publishing Expert, Founder of Ignite Press

 https://www.linkedin.com/company/ignite-press (Company)

 https://www.linkedin.com/in/everettokeefe/ (Personal)

 https://www.facebook.com/ignitepress

 https://IgnitePress.us

Everett O'Keefe is an International #1 Bestselling Author, having authored six Amazon #1 bestselling books. He has also helped create and launch more than 65 bestselling books for his clients. Everett speaks across the nation on the power of publishing. He is the founder of Ignite Press, a hybrid publishing company that specializes in helping entrepreneurs, as well as business and medical professionals, ignite their businesses by becoming bestselling authors.

Everett is the winner of multiple awards, including the Publish and Profit Award for Excellence in Publishing, the Make Market & Launch It Award for Product Creation, and the Top Gun Consulting Award, among others. He is the co-founder of the Business Accelerator Group, a high-level mastermind group composed of international marketers and publishers. He also founded the Book Publishers Network as well as The Mastermind Retreat.

Everett is sought out as a speaker, coach, and consultant by authors and marketing experts worldwide. With a passion for entrepreneurialism, Everett helps his clients become recognized experts in their fields through speaking and authorship while allowing his clients to focus on their own areas of giftedness. You may find Everett's latest book, The Power of the Published, wherever books are sold.

> *"Give me a lever and a place to stand,*
> *and I will move the earth."*

— ARCHIMEDES

In physics, a force multiplier is something that increases the effect of a force. Perhaps the most obvious example is a lever and fulcrum. Archimedes, the Greek mathematician, philosopher, and engineer, claimed that all it took was a solid place to stand and a long enough lever, and he could move anything. The same thing is true when working on cars. The most stubborn nut will turn with ease if you have a wrench with a long enough handle. Archimedes' lever and the long wrench of the mechanic are force multipliers. They quite literally *multiply* the amount of force that can be exerted.

As you will see, books are the ultimate force multiplier for a business or brand. Because of the authority they create, they can have a profound and lasting impact on your business. Let's explore why.

CELEBRITY STATUS

Although it is easier than ever to become an author, especially with self- and hybrid-publishing, there are few people we regard more highly than authors. We may respect doctors, pastors, teachers, and counselors, but these often pale in comparison to authors. Maybe it is simply because we encounter authors far less frequently than we do people in these other professions. I suspect it is really because of our attachment to celebrities.

Authors have been considered celebrities for centuries, and arguably, millennia. This is still true today. Consider George R. R. Martin, Maya Angelou, Stephen King, Malcolm Gladwell, John Maxwell, Dan Sullivan, Og Mandino, Tony Robbins, Tim Ferris, Seth Godin, etc. All of these individuals have become celebrities by writing or increased their celebrity status through writing.

Interestingly, not only are popular writers celebrities, but they actually are among our most revered celebrities. While the headlines are filled with the travails and moral failings of politicians, professional athletes, and radio/television stars, authors largely have been left unsullied by tabloid journalism.

In our society, we grant great authority to celebrities. While one can argue why this is the case, the number of paid celebrity endorsements demonstrates how powerful this celebrity status is in marketing. The mere authoring of a book imparts a certain celebrity status. With authorship, *you* can be the celebrity in your network, and *you* can enjoy the authority that comes with it. This celebrity status is just one reason books are the ultimate force multiplier.

CO-CREATION

Books are a unique medium and one that allows the author and the reader to create together. Think about when you read a book. You only see lines and dots on a page. These coalesce in your mind to become words and thoughts. You start to form images in your head. In books, the writer shares stories, examples, and information, and our mind takes this data and allows it to combine and solidify inside our minds. The space between the details leaves room for us to add our own ideas and interpretations. Soon, the story in our mind is as much *our* creation as it is that of the writer. We have become *co-creators* with the author, and this allows us to subconsciously take ownership of the content.

What's more, as Brendon Burchard likes to point out, "People support what they create." When we have a hand in the creation of something, we take a stake in it. We want to see it succeed, and we are naturally biased toward it. When we read a book and co-create with the author, we are naturally disposed to believe the story we helped create. As a result, we are more accepting of what we read in a book than what is presented verbally or even visually. This makes books incredibly powerful as a tool for marketing and expert positioning.

LONG-FORM COMMUNICATION

We are swayed by the long-form nature of a book. In this world of 30-second commercials and five-second sound bites, the mere act of spending a few hours with a book opens our minds in a way that is hard to duplicate with any other media. The relationship between the writer and the reader is a very intimate thing. The writer can guide the reader through stories, facts, and opinions, moving the reader this way and that, spending literally hours together in the process. By the end of the book, having devoted so much time together, the reader feels connected to the writer in a way that just cannot occur within a normal business setting.

Ask yourself this: *'How much time do you get to spend with your typical client or prospect? How much time do you have to convince prospects that they need your services?'* If you are like most people, you may have only minutes (or just moments!) to sway a prospective customer. Not so with books. If you can put your book in the hands of clients and prospects, they may spend *hours* learning from you. Rather than being on guard while listening to a pitch in your office, your prospects will take you home with them. They will read your book while sitting on the couch and lounging around the pool. They will probably even take you to bed with them! Your clients and prospects will be listening to you, learning from you during their most relaxed and vulnerable moments. This gives you, the author, an advantage unlike any other.

THE POWER OF THE UNREAD BOOK

Unfortunately, a large percentage of those who receive a copy of your book will never read it. This is a sad reality. Take a look at your own bookshelf. Whether at home or work, my guess is you have many books that you purchased or were given to you that you intended to read someday, but just have not gotten around to reading.

Think of the books you own, but have not read. Consider the authors. How do you feel about them? Is your opinion of them somehow lessened, because you have not yet read their book? Or do you consider the authors to be authorities simply because they have written a book? The mere presence of these books on your bookshelf, desk, or nightstand continually reinforces the expert status of each of the authors. Every time you see an author's name on the cover, his or her authority is reinforced, even though you have not read the book.

It has long been my opinion that 95% of those who will be influenced by your book will never read it. I have no studies to back up this claim. Yet, while the percentage may be slightly off, I know I am in the ballpark.

The truth is this. Most people will never read your book. *But,* most people who encounter your book in some way or another *will* be influenced by it. They may only hear the title or see the cover or even simply learn you have written a book, and they will be moved by it. If people know you have written a book on a specific topic, they will be predisposed to consider you an authority or expert on the topic. There is incredible power in the unread book!

DURABLE MARKETING

Most marketing is very short-lived. An ad in a daily newspaper is only useful as long as the prospect is looking at the page upon which it is printed. A social media post (paid or otherwise) is seen once and is then gone.

There are more durable marketing techniques. Wherever you are reading this book, look around. Do you have a pen or coffee mug with some company's logo on it? How about a mouse pad, cell phone holder, desk calendar, clock, refrigerator magnet, or any other promotional item? These items are designed to provide repeat brand exposure and increase name recognition. The sad truth is that, while these items are durable, they impart no credibility or authority, and they often are ignored or quickly discarded.

Not so with books!

Books are the ultimate durable marketing product. They outlast any other marketing strategy of which I can think because people don't throw them away! Look at the books you own. How long have you held onto these books? How many *years* have you held on to them?

Frankly, I think many of us are uncomfortable with the destruction or discarding of books. Maybe this is because we understand there is intrinsic value in books due to the wisdom they contain. Or, maybe it is FOMO (fear of missing out) that makes us hold onto books we may never read.

Either way, if people, in general, have this deep-seated aversion to the destruction of books, why not put this to work for you? Books have such longevity that many copies will outlast your clients... or you. Your book even has the potential to be handed down from generation to generation. Can you say that about any other marketing product?

THE ORIGINAL VIRAL MARKETING

Before there were funny YouTube videos, there were books! And, they were shared. They still are! We still talk to people about the books we are reading, and sometimes we share books among our friends and associates. Books really are the original viral marketing medium. Books have helped people share religions and political ideologies for millennia. Their durable nature and their long-format communication style have made them effective methods of communication for most of recorded history.

So, a book is both durable *and* viral. This is why a book is the ultimate durable marketing piece. There is nothing like a book to provide an enduring and impactful marketing message for years and decades to come. In fact, once written and published, your book can impact your business for the rest of your life and perhaps beyond. It is one of the very few things you will create in your life that will outlive you.

THE INFLUENTIAL WHISPER

A book is like a trusted friend who whispers advice in your ear. While you are considering your choices, he tells you in which direction to go. Because you respect your friend so much, you give great credence to his advice. While you won't blindly follow his direction, you value his opinion above almost all others.

When you read a book, this trusted friend continually tells you that the author is wise and to be trusted. He tells you the author's statements are likely to be true. This "influential whisper" is continuously present, subtly affecting you as you read every page.

Perhaps this is so, due to the long format of a book or because the reader is co-creating with the author. Maybe it is that people read books when their defenses are down, or they read a book in multiple sittings, creating the spaced repetition that is so powerful in marketing. Whatever the reason, books exert power and impact, unlike any other marketing tool.

***

In this chapter, I have listed only a few of the reasons that a book is a force multiplier for your business or organization. Whether we are talking about the durable nature of books, the unique influencing power of a book, or even the power of the *unread* book, it is easy to see the impact a book can have. Because of these reasons and the authority that authorship imparts, a book multiplies the power of its author. Whether your goal is to increase the profits of your business or to amplify the message you have for the world, a book is the most powerful tool you can choose.

Do you have a book that you've written?

If not, have you considered writing one?

Reach out to us. We would be happy to discuss how to put the ultimate force multiplier to work for you.

Just visit https://IgnitePress.us to arrange a complimentary book consultation.

CHAPTER 15

Why Should Authors Make an Audiobook?

Founder, Gutenberg Reloaded

https://www.facebook.com/GutenbergReloaded

https://www.youtube.com/channel/UCF_9iLkvxcYlv-c_PcKP50Q

www.gutenbergreloaded.com

George Smolinski founded Gutenberg Reloaded in 2012 after starting his publishing journey with his twin sons. After helping them create their own book when they were only six years old, he quickly realized the power and potential of Kindle publishing.

Moving forward, his company worked to specialize in audiobook production, a key component of any publishing or authority strategy and today runs Gutenberg Reloaded in cooperation with his wife Amy, a voice actor and authority herself!

T he answer to whether authors should make an audiobook is fairly straightforward and fits right in with the theme of this book: an audiobook gives an author *authority* and I aim to explain exactly how it does so in a bit.

First, a little about audiobooks in general. Millions of audiobook listeners worldwide consume audiobooks at a very rapid clip, and therefore, the business case for audiobooks makes sense. The statistics are quite dramatic: according to the Audio Publishers Association, the average year-over-year growth of the audiobook market recently has ranged from 25%-35%, whereas the year-over-year growth of the eBook market has been in the single digits.

The incredible aspect of this growth is that there seems to be no end in sight, as these strong growth trends have been present for years. Formats for listening to audio change with time, (remember mix tapes and eight-track players?), but the combination of smartphones, MP3s, and busy lives have yielded fertile ground for audiobook growth.

Aside from those statistics, however, audio does something a "regular" book cannot: audio brings your book to life. A strong subset of readers actually prefer audiobook content above all other ways of consuming content, and for a good reason: a well-narrated audiobook brings another dimension to your book. It's the same reason why movie versions of books are so incredibly popular — the book itself is brought to life. Audio does much of the same.

More and more people are choosing to take in content via audio as their *preferred way of content consumption.* As such, in order to broadcast your message with the widest possible net, you need to ensure that you are reaching your customers through their ears, as well as their eyes.

But, back to the authority aspect of audiobooks — how does an audiobook establish your authority? The answer lies in the fact that the quality standards needed for audiobooks are much higher than just with eBooks, and obviously being in the company of high-quality colleagues immediately establishes *you* as being high quality as well! Let's go back a few years to the advent of Amazon's Kindle Direct Publishing platform.

This platform caused the entire book publishing industry to be turned on its head. In the days before Amazon, if an author hoped to publish their book, they relied on just that — hope. It's said that J.K. Rowling's original Harry Potter script was "saved" by the eight-year-old daughter of the publishing company's CEO recommending it as a good read and the rest is history. Indeed, the old system had its flaws (think of the stories just like Harry Potter that *weren't* published!), but it did serve one purpose — your story had to be really great (and you had to have luck) to even get noticed.

With the advent of Kindle Direct Publishing, all of a sudden anyone could publish a book. The barrier to entry in publishing was eliminated, and the eBook market exploded. The democratization of the field was good for authors, but with the big caveat that a lot of poorly written books flooded the market. As time went on, that has improved somewhat, but there still is virtually no barrier to publishing an eBook, which has yielded some very poor quality books being published on Kindle.

With audiobooks, however, the underlying quality of the book and the actual audio files themselves must be high quality. To publish an audiobook, an author first must have the financial resources to create the audiobook. The cost is not astronomical, but it's still enough to deter many brand-new authors — especially those with rather poor quality content. Second, the audio production itself must be of high quality for the book to be accepted on the Audiobook

Creation Exchange (ACX), which then distributes the audiobook to Amazon, Audible, and iTunes. With Kindle Direct Publishing, as long as a book meets the technical specifications of an eBook (which are as simple as having a Word document plus a .JPG book cover), the book can be published. Not so with ACX. On that platform, the audio files actually are reviewed by hand in a two-step process to ensure listeners will have a good experience while listening to the audiobook. If the files sound poorly or have errors in them, the book simply won't be accepted for publication. This eliminates a significant number of poorly recorded audiobooks. Furthermore, if an author *does* have a poor-quality book, but decides to spend a significant amount of money to get it recorded, then the book will immediately get poor reviews on Audible. Because audiophiles are so passionate about the medium, book reviews on Audible truly can be brutal, which further tamps down poor quality content. Given all these factors, if you can get your book created into an audiobook, then you're automatically included amongst higher quality content offerings, and this builds your authority simply by your inclusion!

So, you're now faced with a scenario of having a content-distribution platform (ACX) that is populated with high-quality content and is experiencing tremendous growth. This is normally a great scenario for positive returns on investments, but there's an even more powerful reason for creating an audiobook, specifically pertaining to the consumer profile of audiobook listeners. Audiobook consumers tend to be better educated and have a higher net worth than eBook consumers. Why is this important? If you're using your book to build your brand and help your business grow, of course, you're going to want to attract potential clients and customers with a higher net worth, especially if you're a small business. So often small businesses cannot compete on quantity, so they must establish themselves as authoritative experts and seek out clients, as well as customers with a high net worth — audiobooks complement this business strategy perfectly.

HOW TO CREATE AN AUDIOBOOK

Having established how an audiobook positions you as an authority, it's certainly worth covering exactly how an audiobook is created and answering common questions pertaining to audiobook production. The most common question pertaining to audiobook production is: how difficult is it to create an audiobook? Essentially there are two options for creating an audiobook and we have helped hundreds of authors worldwide with both options. First, and perhaps the simplest, is to have it professionally recorded.

Having a professional voice actor record your audiobook is an excellent option for busy professionals, and it involves simply sending your script to a voice actor or a company like ours (Gutenberg Reloaded, www.gutenbergreloaded.com) that produces audiobooks and then they deliver upload-ready audio files compliant with ACX standards. Of course, they'll be responsible for all the editing and engineering of the files, so you have a great sounding audiobook. Any voice actor worth their salt will know exactly how to accomplish that with an audio engineer and they'll have the skillset to deliver a great-sounding audiobook.

The second option is to do it yourself. Many authors think that this is a tremendous undertaking, but it's not quite as intimidating as it might seem. Normally, with a little education, training, and around $100 of recording equipment, a new author can produce a good sounding audiobook. Of course, not *everyone* has a pleasing voice, and we advise anyone considering this route to send us files to review BEFORE they try and record hours of audio. We also advise them to have an honest friend or two assess their voice and give honest feedback.

However, if the author sounds good on the mic, they usually can create a good recording, set up in a small closet in their house, and get their book recorded in a weekend. It's important to note that the normal rate of human speech is about 8,000 words per hour, so one easily can extrapolate how long it would take to record their audiobook based on word count. Also important, there are outtakes, breaks, and so forth, that increase the recording time.

Having recorded my own audiobook (aptly titled *Recording Audiobooks*) I can say that it's rather tiring as well. With all those factors, however, many authors still feel that it's important to voice their own work to truly "make it their own" and usually, the obstacles incumbent with recording their own audiobook are not too great to overcome.

Once the audio is recorded, the next step is choosing where to sell it. This also is a very common question posed to us. Quite simply, the answer is ACX. Granted, there are other audiobook platforms out there and people can sell their audiobooks on their own website (even with ACX).

But, if you want to reach Amazon, Audible, and iTunes altogether, the choice is clear: ACX, as they control roughly 85% of the audiobook market share. The process of uploading the audiobook files is not terribly complex, and once submitted, ACX performs a quality control check as aforementioned. This process takes several weeks to complete, and when done, the author receives an email notification that their audiobook is for sale.

In summary, when an author or a business owner is looking to garner more readers or attract more clients and customers, they absolutely must prove themselves as an authority in today's hyper-competitive world. Audiobooks make perfect sense then, as they themselves tend to be high quality and the audiobook consumer is typically one with a higher net worth and more education.

Whether it's recording the audiobook yourself or having it professionally produced, an audiobook makes perfect sense for anyone looking to establish their authority.

Lastly, this chapter only covers the surface of the world of audiobook production, and has produced more than 500 audiobooks, we have covered every possible scenario involved.

As such, if you have any questions whatsoever about producing an audiobook, please feel free to reach out to us at contact@ gutenbergreloaded.com, and we're happy to assist. Best of luck to you with establishing *your* authority!

Conclusion

T hank you for joining us in this conversation about what it means to have authority, along with the many ways to acquire and increase authority in business, as well as everyday life. As you have seen, the methods of creating authority are varied and involve almost any medium. While increased authority produces diverse results, they universally are positive and can have a dramatic impact on a business, brand, and life.

We hope that your life will be impacted by *Authority*. For this to happen, you must go deeper and take action. Reach out to one or more of the authors in this book. Take advantage of the resources they offer. Learn from and engage with them to increase *your* authority.

Someone is waiting to *learn* from you. Someone is waiting to be *inspired* by you.

The unique combination of knowledge and life experience you possess equips you to teach or inspire that person in a way unlike any other individual. Without you, he or she may never hear the message they so desperately need to make improvements in life. Step into your role as an authority. Embrace it so that the world, or maybe just that one person, may be changed.

CPSIA information can be obtained
at www.ICGtesting.com
Printed in the USA
BVHW061014140121
597841BV00010B/545